A PRACTICAL GUIDE TO FINANCIAL MANAGEMENT

A PRACTICAL GUIDE TO FINANCIAL MANAGEMENT

Tips and techniques for the non-financial manager

Michael M. Coltman

SELF-COUNSEL SERIES

International Self-Counsel Press Ltd.
Vancouver Toronto

Self-Counsel Press Inc.
Seattle

Printed in Canada

Printed in Canada

First edition: November, 1984

Cataloguing in Publication Data:
Coltman, Michael M. (Michael Macdonald), 1930-
A practical guide to financial management

(Self-Counsel series)
ISBN 0-88908-600-1

1. Small business — Finance. I. Title.
II. Series.
HG4027.7.C65 1984 658.1'592 C84-091394-X

SELF-COUNSEL SERIES

International Self-Counsel Press Ltd.
Editorial Office
306 West 25th Street,
North Vancouver,
British Columbia V7N 2G1
Canada

Self-Counsel Press Inc.
1303 N. Northgate Way,
Seattle,
Washington, 98133 U.S.A.
(a subsidiary of International Self-Counsel Press Ltd.)

CONTENTS

LIST OF SAMPLES

1
INTRODUCTION

The purpose of this book is to discuss and illustrate some practical ideas and methods that will improve the profitability of any small business that wishes to become more effective in the management of its financial affairs.

a. SMALL BUSINESS DEFINITION

What is a small business? There are many definitions, but many of them are meaningless, particularly when expressed in terms of annual sales dollars, or number of persons employed. Perhaps the best description is that which defines a small business as one that is independently owned and operated and not dominant in its field of endeavor.

Most small businesses are established to manufacture, distribute, and retail an inordinate variety of goods and services. Despite the fact that the large corporations receive much press and publicity, most are dependent on small business. For example, companies that mass produce manufactured goods could not possibly distribute them without the myriad of small firms that handle transportation, wholesaling, and retailing. In other words, small business enterprises constitute the backbone of free enterprise economies.

b. SKILLS REQUIRED

Traditionally, the level of management skills has been considerably less in small businesses than in larger ones, but the market that these small businesses face is just as complex as that to which large corporations are exposed.

The small business entrepreneur needs basically the same management skills as a manager in a large business. They both must plan and prepare strategies for the future. In addition, they must solve problems, resolve priorities, determine policies, and make financial decisions on a daily basis. Operating results must be constantly analyzed, and outside factors that may have an effect on the internal operations of the business must be considered.

However, the individual small business owner must assume a wider range of responsibilities than the general manager of a large corporation. The manager of a large corporation will have vice-presidents for finance, for marketing, for manufacturing and production, for distribution, and so on. Each of these vice-presidents has important responsibilities, but each is concerned with only one specific area of the total company activities.

In a small business, the owner generally has a daily responsibility for all of the above as well as for ongoing problems concerning personnel, inventory, sales, credit, suppliers, new policy implementation, new product introductions, public relations, marketing, and financial reporting.

In recent years, even the best managed businesses have found it difficult to maintain, let alone improve, their profits. It has also become increasingly difficult for them to pass on price and labor cost increases to their customers in the way of increased product or service prices.

The only way they can compensate for their own cost increases is to reduce employees, reduce other operating expenses, improve productivity, or practice better financial management. All of this has to be attempted without affecting the established quality of the service and or products.

c. RISK INVOLVED

Those who go into small business do so in spite of, or in ignorance of, the odds of survival. A rule of thumb for new small businesses is that as many as 50% fail during the first year, and as many as 90% in less than five years.

Statistical analyses of business failures show that as many as 95% of these failures are caused by lack of competence and managerial experience in that particular business.

In addition, small business failures are said to be caused by any or all of the following specific problems:

(a) Inability to find competent employees
(b) Inadequate starting capital
(c) Inability to finance expansion
(d) Poor sales because of low demand for the product or service
(e) High operating expenses
(f) Limited credit from suppliers
(g) Shortage of working capital
(h) Poor location
(i) Inability to make a new product known to the market
(j) Impossible tax burdens
(k) Failure to formulate plans and objectives
(l) Pressure from large competitors with a vested interest to see the business fail
(m) Inability to keep proper financial records

You will notice that many of the items mentioned in this list relate to financial factors. In fact, most aspects of a business are eventually reflected in one way or another in the financial statements.

The small business owner's ability to practice more effective financial management will be subsequently reflected by improved results recorded in the financial statements.

Many small business owners have skills in areas other than financial management. This book is for those non-financial managers who see the need to improve the financial management of their business, but need some practical help on how to do it. When you have finished this book, you should have learned enough to be able to plan your financial management with much greater precision and effectiveness in order to maximize your profits.

Some of the financial management problems you may suffer from are: having insufficient working capital, improper management of working capital, obtaining the wrong type of financing, obtaining it at the wrong time, over- or under-estimating the amount needed, or not understanding the true cost of borrowing money.

Effective financial management is even more important in times of tight money and inflation where the small business owner does not have the financial resources of its larger competitors. For example, in such times investors and lenders are more difficult to find and when they can be found it may not be as easy to get a foot in the door and even less easy to negotiate favorable borrowing terms.

d. YOUR FINANCIAL OBJECTIVES

Every business has money that it must manage. This money comes from creditors (such as bankers) who lend the company money and from owners who do likewise, or who purchase shares in the company. This money can be kept in the business in liquid form (cash), or in interest bearing bank deposits. It can be tied up in inventories or in accounts receivable, or it can be invested in long-term assets such as land and buildings or equipment and fixtures.

At any time, a balance sheet will give you a picture of your business's financial position. A later balance sheet will show a different financial position, since no ongoing business can remain financially static.

Money is constantly going into and out of the business, and the mix between the various sources of money, and its various uses, is always changing. This mixing of sources and uses, according to some established plan, is what financial management is all about. In a small business the owner/manager is the coordinator of that financial plan or set of financial objectives.

In summary, the purposes of financial management are:

(a) To establish certain goals such as how large the business will be, how it will expand and how rapidly, and how success in meeting those goals will be measured

(b) To create a plan for obtaining the money necessary to meet the business's goals
(c) To allocate that money to the various assets of the business, again keeping the company's goals in mind.

e. OBJECTIVES OF YOUR BUSINESS

In order for you to make meaningful decisions about your sources and uses of money, you must first establish some objectives to do with business size and growth rate, and how this will be measured. Only with clearly stated objectives can you effectively manage your company's finances.

An objective can be stated quite simply. For example, the owner/operator of a very small company might have as an objective to make enough profit in 11 months to close the business for a month's holiday each year.

As companies become larger, and have more employees, objectives become more formalized, and sometimes more complex.

1. Profit maximization

A common objective of many companies is to make the most amount of money in the shortest possible time. This is referred to as profit maximization. The time element is important in profit maximization. For example, you would probably agree that $100,000 profit in year one, and nothing in each of the following nine years, is preferable to $10,000 profit a year for each of the next ten years. Since money has a time value, you would be better to take the $100,000 now, put it into interest bearing or dividend yielding investments, and continue to maximize your profit.

However, one of the problems with profit maximization as a goal is that you may ignore the risks involved. For example, you could maximize your profits by rapidly expanding into a chain of small businesses and then find your financial and human resources are spread so thin that profit goes down instead of up! Is the potential of an immediate profit increase worth the long-term risk?

In other words, with profit maximization as a goal, short-run investments are made while ignoring potentially more profitable long-run alternatives.

2. Return on investment maximization

A variation of the profit maximization objective is maximizing return on your investment. Initially, and particularly for a one-person company, these two objectives may seem like the same thing. However, this is not necessarily the case.

For example, it is possible by financial leverage to rearrange financing in such a way that the amount of profit a company has can be changed (even downward) but the return on the owner's own investment increased. (See chapter 2 for how this works.)

Also, in larger companies with several owners, dividend policies can change an individual owner's return on investment. (Dividends are discussed in chapter 5.)

Further, if your objective is maximization of return on investment, when opportunities arise you must consider alternatives. You might then find that expanding the business to increase sales and profits may be "profitable" (measured by profit maximization) but less "profitable" than the present level of business since overall return on your investment will decline.

Therefore, for most companies, maximization of the owner's return on investment is preferable to maximizing profits.

3. Other goals

Effective financial management must also take into account social goals. Social objectives or responsibilities include such matters as:

(a) Protecting the customer who buys your company's goods or services
(b) Following equitable hiring practices
(c) Paying fair wages
(d) Supporting further education and training of employees

(e) Having a concern about environmental factors

For example, if you run a retail store it is socially responsible to sweep the sidewalk or shovel the snow in front of the door. Since there is usually a cost associated with social objectives, they may conflict with your financial objectives.

However, some social objectives, even with that cost, may improve profits since potential customers of your retail business will notice that you sweep or shovel snow (where other companies do not) and may provide you with business for that reason.

2

FINANCIAL RATIO ANALYSIS

One of the keys to successful financial management is your ability to monitor your business through financial ratio analysis. This chapter is concerned with showing you how to calculate and make meaning out of the most common ratios that are of value to a small business. To do this we will use the hypothetical information from the balance sheet and income statement for Harry's Wholesale Ltd. (See Samples #1 and #2.)

a. CURRENT RATIO

The current ratio is one of the most commonly used ratios to measure a small business's liquidity or its ability to meet its short-term debts (current liabilities) without difficulty. The equation for this ratio is:

$$\frac{\text{Current assets}}{\text{Current liabilities}}$$

Using the numbers from Harry's balance sheet (Sample #1) the ratio is:

$$\frac{\$132{,}000}{\$108{,}000} = 1.22$$

The ratio shows that for every $1.00 of short-term debt (current liabilities) there is $1.22 of current assets. A rule of thumb is that there should be $2.00 or more of current assets for each $1.00 of current liabilities.

However, some businesses can frequently operate with a current ratio of less than 2 to 1. Each business must determine what its most effective current ratio is in order to have a current ratio position that neither creates short-term liquidity problems (too low a ratio) nor sacrifices profitability for safety (too high a ratio). If the ratio is too high, you have too much money tied up in working capital (current assets less current liabilities) that is not earning a profit.

SAMPLE #1
BALANCE SHEET

HARRY'S WHOLESALE LTD.
Balance Sheet as at December 31, 198-

ASSETS			LIABILITIES & OWNER'S EQUITY		
Current assets:			Current liabilities:		
Cash	$ 15,000		Accounts payable	$ 56,000	
Accounts receivable	85,000		Accrued expenses	4,000	
Inventory	27,000		Income tax payable	22,000	
Prepaid expenses	5,000		Current mortgage payable	26,000	
Total current assets		$132,000	Total current liabilities		$108,000
Fixed assets:			Long-term liability:		
Land	$ 61,000		Mortgage payable		487,000
Building	882,000		Total liabilities		$595,000
Equipment	246,000				
	$1,189,000		Owner's equity:		
Accumulated depreciation	(422,000)		Common shares	$200,000	
Total fixed assets		767,000	Retained earnings	104,000	
		$899,000	Total owner's equity		304,000
					$899,000

SAMPLE #2
INCOME STATEMENT

HARRY'S WHOLESALE LTD. Income Statement for Year Ending December 31, 198-	
Sales	$956,000
Cost of goods sold	521,000
Gross profit	$435,000
Operating expenses	303,000
Profit before interest	$132,000
Interest expense	52,000
Profit before income tax	$80,000
Income tax	40,000
Net profit	$ 40,000

b. QUICK RATIO

Since there are some not very liquid assets included in the calculation of the current ratio, bankers and other lenders frequently like to calculate the quick or acid test ratio. The acid test ratio has as its numerator only the cash and accounts receivable:

$$\frac{\text{Cash + receivables}}{\text{Current liabilities}}$$

Harry's ratio is:

$$\frac{\$85{,}000 + \$15{,}000}{\$108{,}000} = 0.93$$

Lenders, under normal circumstances, like to see this ratio at 1 to 1 or higher. In our case it is 0.93 to 1, or less than what is normally considered an acceptable level.

c. ACCOUNTS RECEIVABLE

Many small businesses run into financial and cash flow difficulties because they lose control over their accounts receivable. There are a couple of useful ratios for assessing the situation as far as receivables are concerned. One of these is the calculation of the accounts receivable turnover, and the other is the calculation of the number of days sales tied up in receivables.

1. Accounts receivable turnover

The accounts receivable turnover is calculated as follows:

$$\frac{\text{Credit sales for year}}{\text{Accounts receivable}}$$

Harry looked at the sales on his income statement (all sales were made on a credit basis) and the accounts receivable on his balance sheet. His turnover ratio is:

$$\frac{\$956,000}{\$85,000} = 11.25 \text{ times}$$

In a typical business that allows a 30-day limit for payment of accounts and collects its accounts close to this time limit, an annual turnover of 12 would be acceptable. Harry is close to that limit. If the turnover were higher than 12 this would be acceptable. However, if it were much lower, this would normally not be considered good.

2. Days sales in receivables

Another way of assessing the receivables situation is to calculate the days sales outstanding in receivables. This requires two steps. First you must calculate the average daily credit sales:

$$\frac{\text{Credit sales for year}}{260}$$

The figure of 260 is used as the denominator since Harry is running a wholesale business and it is assumed it is open for 5 days a week for 52 weeks in a year. If the business were a retail one open 6 days a week, the appropriate denominator would be 52 x 6 or 312, and if the business were open 7 days a week (for example, a restaurant), then the denominator would be 365.

In Harry's case:

$$\frac{\$956,000}{260} = \$3,677 \text{ per day}$$

The next step is to calculate the average number of days that the year end accounts receivable figure (from the balance sheet) represents. The equation for this is:

$$\frac{\text{Accounts receivable at year end}}{\text{Average daily credit sales}}$$

Harry's calculations are:

$$\frac{\$85,000}{\$3,677} = 23 \text{ days}$$

Note that Harry's figure of 23 days is "working" days and would be the equivalent of about a calendar month.

Whenever the accounts receivable results indicate that the turnover rate or number of days outstanding are over the desirable limit of, let us say, 30 calendar days, you need to ask and answer the following typical questions:

(a) Can the business carry these overdue accounts without impairing its cash position?
(b) Is a 30-day limit normal for our type of business?
(c) Have we been unwise in extending more than 30 days' credit to some customers?
(d) Can anything be done to encourage more prompt payment of outstanding accounts?
(e) Would an interest charge on overdue accounts speed up collections?
(f) Has the bad debt loss amount increased because some customers do not pay within the normal 30-day limit?

d. INVENTORY TURNOVER

The amount of cash tied up in inventory can, at times, be as serious as money tied up in overdue accounts receivable. One measure of the acceptability of the inventory level is the inventory turnover calculation:

$$\frac{\text{Cost of goods sold}}{\text{Average inventory}}$$

Average inventory is normally defined as: (beginning of the year inventory + end of the year inventory) divided by 2.

Harry's inventory figure from his balance sheet is the average figure. His turnover rate would then be:

$$\frac{\$521{,}000}{\$27{,}000} = 19.3 \text{ times for the year}$$

This is a little more than 1-½ times a month. You must try to determine what the normal or standard inventory turnover rate is for your particular type of business and watch for deviations of your turnover from this standard.

e. TOTAL LIABILITIES TO TOTAL EQUITY RATIO

The total assets in a business can be financed by either liabilities (debt) or equity (shares and retained earnings). The total liabilities to total equity ratio (commonly called the debt to equity ratio) illustrates the relationship between these two forms of financing. It is calculated as follows:

$$\frac{\text{Total liabilities}}{\text{Total owner's equity}}$$

Harry's figures are:

$$\frac{\$595{,}000}{\$304{,}000} = 1.96$$

This ratio tells Harry that for each $1.00 that he has invested, the creditors, or lenders, have invested $1.96. The higher the creditors' ratio, or debt to equity ratio, the higher is the risk to the creditor or lender. In such circumstances, if a business needed additional money to expand its operations, it might find it difficult to borrow the funds.

While your creditors prefer not to have the debt to equity ratio too high, you will often find it more profitable to have it as high as possible. A high debt to equity ratio is known as having high leverage. Using leverage, or trading on the equity, will be discussed later in this chapter.

f. NUMBER OF TIMES INTEREST EARNED

Another measure that creditors sometimes use to measure the safety of their investment is the number of times interest is earned during a year. The equation for this is:

$$\frac{\text{Profit before interest and income tax}}{\text{Interest expense}}$$

Harry's figures are:

$$\frac{\$132{,}000}{\$52{,}000} = 2.54 \text{ times}$$

Generally an investor or creditor considers the investment safe if interest is earned two or more times a year.

g. RETURN ON ASSETS

Lenders also sometimes like to calculate the return on assets. The equation for this is:

$$\frac{\text{Profit before interest and income tax}}{\text{Total assets}}$$

In Harry's case the result is:

$$\frac{\$132,000}{\$899,000} = .147 \text{ or } 14.7\%$$

This result can then be compared with current interest rates on borrowed money. For example, a lender from whom Harry wanted to borrow money to expand his business might have a 15% current interest rate. If the expanded premises resulted in additional profits before interest and income tax of only 14.7%, the lender might question whether Harry's business can even meet the additional interest payments.

h. NET PROFIT TO ASSETS

As an alternative to borrowing money for expansion Harry could lend money to the business. The net profit to assets ratio will give him some idea of the return he could expect. The equation is:

$$\frac{\text{Net profit}}{\text{Total assets}}$$

Harry's present profit to assets figures are:

$$\frac{\$40,000}{\$899,000} = 0.044 \text{ or } 4.4\%$$

If that were the return on any additional investment, Harry might be better off to leave his money in the bank in a no-risk savings account since it likely will earn quite a bit more than 4.4%.

i. NET PROFIT TO SALES RATIO

When Harry wanted to measure his profitability, he used the common measure of net profit to sales ratio:

$$\frac{\text{Net profit}}{\text{Sales}} \times 100$$

His figures are:

$$\frac{\$40,000}{\$956,000} \times 100 = 4.2\%$$

Harry saw that out of each $1.00 of sales there were 4.2¢ net profit. The net profit to sales ratio of many businesses falls in the range of 3% to 7% (there are exceptions to this guideline). In absolute terms these percentages may not be too meaningful, because they do not necessarily truly represent the profitability of the business. Consider the following two cases:

	Business A	Business B
Sales	$100,000	$100,000
Net profit	5,000	10,000
Net profit to sales ratio	5%	10%

With the same sales it seems that Business B is better. Business B is making twice as much net profit, in absolute terms, as is Business A ($10,000 to $5,000). This doubling of net profit is supported by the net profit to sales ratio (10% to 5%).

If these were two similar businesses, or two branches of the same business, these figures would indicate the relative effectiveness of the management of each in controlling costs and generating a satisfactory level of profit. However, in order to determine the profitability of a small business you need to relate the net profit to the investment by calculating the return on the owners' equity or return on investment.

j. RETURN ON OWNER'S EQUITY

The equation for return on owner's equity is:

$$\frac{\text{Net profit}}{\text{Owner's equity}} \times 100$$

Harry's figures are:

$$\frac{\$40{,}000}{\$304{,}000} \times 100 = 13.2\%$$

This ratio shows the effectiveness of Harry's use of his own funds (or equity).

How high should the ratio be? This is a matter of personal opinion. If an investor could put money either into the bank at a 10% interest rate or into a business investment at only 8%, with more risk involved, the bank might look like the better of the two choices. Many people feel that 15% (after tax) is a reasonable return for the owner of a small business (with all its risks) to expect.

Now we can return to the Business A and Business B situation discussed earlier. Assume that the investment in A was $40,000 and in B $80,000. The return on investment would be:

Business A $$\frac{\$5{,}000}{\$40{,}000} \times 100 = 12.5\%$$

Business B $$\frac{\$10{,}000}{\$80{,}000} \times 100 = 12.5\%$$

Despite the wide difference in net profit, and net profit to sales ratio (calculated earlier), there is no difference between the two businesses as far as profitability is concerned. They are both equally as good, each yielding a 12.5% return on the investment, or return on owner's equity.

k. FINANCIAL LEVERAGE

Alice and Sue are business partners. They are considering leasing a new building for their business. Their investment would be $250,000 for equipment and working capital.

The two partners have the cash available, but they are considering not using all their own money. Instead, they wish to compare their relative return on equity based on using either all their own money (100% equity financing) or using 50% equity and borrowing the other 50% (debt financing) at a 10% interest rate.

Regardless of which financing method they use, sales will be the same, as will all operating costs. With either choice, they will have $50,000 profit before interest and taxes.

There is no interest expense under 100% equity financing. With debt financing interest will have to be paid. However, interest expense is tax deductible.

Sample #3 shows the comparative operating results and the return on the partners' investment (ROI) for each of the two options (assuming a tax rate of 50% on profit).

In this situation not only do Alice and Sue make a better ROI under a 50/50 debt/equity ratio (15% ROI versus 10%), but they still have $125,000 cash that they can invest in a second venture.

Because a 50/50 debt to equity ratio is more profitable than 100% equity financing, Alice and Sue wondered if an 80/20 debt to equity ratio would be even more profitable. In other words, what would the ROI be if they used only $50,000 of their own money, and borrowed the remaining $200,000 at 10%? Sample #4 shows the result of this more highly levered situation.

Under this third option, the return on initial investment has now increased to 30%, and Alice and Sue still have $200,000 cash — enough for four more similar business ventures.

1. Advantages of leverage

The advantages of leverage are obvious: the higher the debt to equity ratio, the higher the ROI. However, this only holds true if profit (before interest) as a percent of debt is greater than the interest rate to be paid on the debt. For example, if the debt interest rate is 10%, the profit before interest must be more than 10% of the money borrowed (the debt) for leverage to be profitable.

SAMPLE #3
EFFECT OF LEVERAGE ON ROI

	100% equity	50% equity 50% debt
Total investment required	$250,000	$250,000
Debt financing at 10%		$125,000
Equity financing	$250,000	125,000
Profit before interest and tax	$ 50,000	$ 50,000
Interest expense 10% × $125 000		(12,500)
Profit before tax	$ 50,000	$37,500
Income tax 50%	(25,000)	(18,750)
Net profit	$ 25,000	$ 18,750
Return on partners' investment	$\frac{\$25,000}{\$250,000} \times 100$ = 10%	$\frac{\$18,750}{\$125,000} \times 100$ = 15%

SAMPLE #4
EFFECT OF HIGH LEVERAGE ON ROI

Total investment required	$250,000
Debt financing at 10%	$200,000
Equity financing	$ 50,000
Profit before interest and tax	$ 50,000
Interest 10% × $200 000	(20,000)
Profit before tax	$ 30,000
Income tax 50%	(15,000)
Net profit	$ 15,000
Return on partners' investment	$\frac{\$15,000}{\$50,000} \times 100$ = 30%

2. Risks of leverage

With high debt (high leverage) there is a risk. If profit declines, the more highly levered the business is, the sooner it will be in financial difficulty. In 50/50 financing (relatively low leverage), profit before interest and income tax could decline from $50,000 to $12,500 before net profit would be zero (see Sample #3). In 80/20 financing (relatively high leverage), profit before interest and income tax could decline from $50,000 to only $20,000 (see Sample #4).

What is the "best" debt to equity ratio for a business? There is no best ratio. The figure differs from one type of business to another, and even between two similar types of business, since there are so many variables to be considered at any particular time. These variables would include the relative profitability of the business, current interest rates, alternative uses for your equity money, the present economic climate, and many others.

However, in general, lenders like to see a debt/equity ratio that is on a par with published debt/equity ratio figures for similar businesses or industries.

3

WORKING CAPITAL MANAGEMENT

The balance sheets of most businesses have a section called current assets. This section includes items such as cash, accounts receivable, marketable securities, inventories, and prepaid expenses. Current assets are generally considered to be items that are cash, or can be converted into cash fairly quickly or in less than a year if necessary.

On the other side of the balance sheet is a section for the current liabilities for such items as accounts payable, accrued expenses, income tax payable, current portion of long-term loans or mortgages, and dividends payable. Current liabilities are debts that have to be paid within the next year. They are generally paid by the cash that normally circulates through a business.

This circulation results from using cash to buy inventory, selling that inventory for cash or on credit (accounts receivable) and collecting cash from the accounts receivable. Since the selling price of items purchased for inventory is greater than their cost a "profit" results, and thus current assets can be used to pay for current liabilities.

However, it is not always that simple. The ability of a business to pay its current liabilities when they are due depends on the amount and timing of cash inflows from cash and credit sales. As long as most sales are for cash, or if credit sales are collected quickly, then there should be sufficient cash to pay for current liabilities. But if you are overstocked with inventory or find it difficult to collect on accounts receivable, cash flow may be troublesome.

a. DEFINITION OF WORKING CAPITAL

The difference between total current assets and total current liabilities is known as working capital.

Current assets — current liabilities = working capital

However, even though working capital is defined as the arithmetical difference between current assets and current liabilities, it is, more importantly, a reflection of the ability of the manager of the business to effectively control each current asset and current liability account given the operating conditions for that business.

The objective is to conserve cash, earn interest on it (one possibility), and thus increase profits and maximize return on investment.

In other words, the amount of working capital required by a business is the amount that results from each current asset and each current liability being at the best level to ensure, for example, that there is sufficient inventory on hand, or that accounts payable are paid when due.

A business with a good working capital position will be able to buy its inventory, supplies, and services on favorable terms and with satisfactory delivery schedules. It will be able to take advantage of trade discounts offered and keep its own prices competitive. It will have a good credit rating and will not be dictated to by its creditors. It will collect its accounts receivable promptly and not suffer high bad debt losses.

b. HOW MUCH WORKING CAPITAL?

How much working capital does a business need? This cannot be answered in general terms with an absolute dollar amount. For example, suppose it were a rule of thumb that a business should have a working capital of $5,000. A business might find itself with the following:

Current assets	$15,000
Current liabilities	10,000
Working capital	$ 5,000

A larger business would have to have larger amounts of cash, inventories, accounts receivable, and other current asset items. Also, it would probably have larger amounts in its various current liability accounts. Its balance sheet might therefore look like this:

Current assets	$100,000
Current liabilities	95,000
Working capital	$ 5,000

The smaller business is in much better financial shape than the larger one. The former has $1.50 ($15,000 divided by $10,000) of current assets for every $1.00 of current liabilities — a comfortable cushion. The latter has just over $1.05 ($100,000 divided by $95,000) of current assets for each dollar of current liabilities — not so comfortable a cushion.

1. General rule

A general rule in business is that a business should preferably have at least $2.00 of current assets for each $1.00 of current liabilities. This would mean that its working capital ($2.00 minus $1.00) is equivalent to its current liabilities.

However, this rule is primarily for companies (such as manufacturing, wholesaling, and some retailing organizations) that need to carry very large inventories that do not turn over rapidly.

Other businesses can operate with a very low ratio of current assets to current liabilities — often as low as 1 to 1. In other words, for each $1 of current assets there is $1 of current liabilities. This means that the business has, in fact, no working capital as defined earlier.

At certain times of the year, some businesses can even operate with negative working capital. In other words, current liabilities will exceed current assets. This might be typical of a business that is seasonal in nature. Such an operation might have current assets vastly in excess of current liabilities during the peak season, and the reverse in the off season.

2. Cash flow

Money does not always come into a business at the same rate as it goes out. At times there will be excess cash on hand; at other times there will be shortages of cash. You need to anticipate both of these events so that shortages can be covered. In this way the cash balance will be kept at its optimum level.

For example, many retail sales businesses, prior to certain peak sales periods, have to borrow large amounts of money to build up their inventories, and tie up working capital, prior to the sale of the products. After the peak sale they may have surplus cash available for a few months prior to the next peak sales period.

In such a situation the peaks and valleys need to be fairly accurately forecast. One of the ways to do this is to be familiar with and properly manage your various working capital accounts such as cash, accounts receivable, marketable securities, and inventory. Good management of these and similar items of working capital will help you generate a good deal of internal financing for your business.

c. CASH

Cash on hand, as distinguished from cash in the bank, is the money in circulation in a business. This could be cash used by cashiers as "floats" or "banks" for making change, petty cash, or just general cash in the safe.

The amount of cash on hand should be sufficient for normal day-to-day operations only. Any surplus idle cash should be deposited in the bank in savings accounts or term deposits so that it can earn interest. Preferably, each day's net cash receipts should be deposited in the bank as soon as possible the following day.

Cash in the bank in a current account should be sufficient to pay only current bills due or current payroll. Any excess funds should be invested in short-term securities (with a good balance between the maximum interest rate and the security and liquidity of the investment) or in savings or other special accounts that earn interest. It may please your bank manager to leave these excess funds in your current account, rather than earn interest on them, but that is not a good business practice.

d. ACCOUNTS RECEIVABLE

Extending credit to your customers is a useful marketing tool to encourage increased sales. However, to maximize this potential you must establish credit policies to ensure your credit system is not so loose that it costs you cash and thus profit.

1. Terms of credit

You need to decide who will be allowed credit and how to determine a customer's credit limit. You also need to decide who has authority to decide who may receive credit and up to what limits. In other words, up to what amount can a customer charge items purchased before credit is no longer extended?

Your terms of credit must also be spelled out for your customers. For example, if you offer a discount off the purchase price for prompt payment of an invoice, what are the discount terms? Also, if full payment is to be made within, let us say, 30 days, is this 30 days from the date of purchase, date of mailing of the invoice, the end of the month following the customer's receipt of the invoice, or some other alternative?

You should make clear to the customer when you expect payment and when you will begin to implement some follow-up procedure. If you don't do this, you may quickly find your cost of extending credit is climbing steeply.

For example, suppose with a 30-day credit limit after purchase of goods your normal balance of accounts receivable is $50,000. If all your customers stretch this to 60 days, your accounts receivable balance will increase to $100,000. That extra $50,000 of credit at a 15% interest rate will increase your cost of doing business by $7,500 a year.

You should ensure that invoices are mailed out promptly and delinquent accounts followed up.

Money tied up in accounts receivable is money not earning a return. Extension of credit to customers is an acknowledged form of business transaction, but it should not be extended to the point of allowing payments to lag two or three months behind the mailing of the invoice. High credit standards can lead to loss of revenue. On the other hand, low standards can lead to bad debts and collection costs.

2. Aging of receivables

A couple of methods of controlling accounts receivable were discussed in chapter 2. Another way of keeping an eye on the accounts receivable is to prepare a chart once a month showing the age of the accounts outstanding. Your chart would look like this:

AGE	MAY 31		JUNE 30	
0-30 days	$59,000	79.5%	$56,400	74.2%
31-60 days	11,800	15.9	8,800	11.6
61-90 days	2,400	3.2	8,600	11.3
over 90 days	1,000	1.4	2,200	2.9
Totals	$74,200	100.0	$76,000	100.0

This chart shows that the accounts receivable outstanding situation has not improved from May to June. In May, 79.5% of total receivables were less than 30 days old. In June, only 74.2% were less than 30 days outstanding. Similarly, the relative percentages in the 31 to 60 day category have worsened from May to June.

By contrast, in the 61 to 90 days bracket, 11.3% of accounts receivable are outstanding in June, against only 3.2% in May.

This particular aging chart shows that the accounts receivable are getting older. If this trend continues, collection procedures will need to be improved. If, after all possible collection procedures have been explored, an account is deemed to be uncollectible, it should be removed from the accounts receivable and recorded as a bad debt expense.

3. Credit cards

Most retail businesses these days accept a variety of credit cards for payment of purchases. You should train your employees to follow established procedures to eliminate losses from such matters as customers purchasing in an amount above their credit card limit, or using stolen or blacklisted credit cards.

Commissions paid to credit card companies can range as high as 6% of your sales on the commercial credit cards (American Express and Diners Club) whereas the commission rate is considerably less on the bank credit cards (Visa and MasterCard). You will also receive the cash from bank credit card sales vouchers the day you deposit them in the bank.

With commercial credit cards, even if you mail the vouchers promptly you might wait two weeks or more before receiving a payment. Your employees should therefore be trained to encourage customers to use bank credit cards rather than commercial ones wherever possible. This will help maximize your profits.

4. Lockboxes

If the volume of your credit sales is large enough, you might also want to consider using a lockbox.

With a lockbox you do not directly collect your own receivables. Instead, customers are directed to send their payment of accounts to a post office box number. Mail from this box is picked up by your bank and the deposits put immediately into your bank account. The bank notifies you each day of the amounts deposited so that you can adjust your accounts receivable records.

The main advantage of the lockbox system is that you gain a day or two on outstanding receivables (and can earn interest on this money).

However, there is a bank cost for using this system, usually in the form of a charge for each receivable check handled. You will need to discuss with your bank manager whether the cost of a lockbox system for your business will exceed the benefits.

5. Deposits

In some businesses it is possible to encourage customers to make payment, or partial payment, by deposit prior to production or delivery of the goods. In other situations, the customer will make payment in stages as work progresses. This reduces the amount that you will be carrying in receivables. In other words, it helps you finance your business and improve your cash flow.

Mail order businesses, custom manufacturers, and building contractors typically require the customer to pay part or all of the purchase price in advance.

e. MARKETABLE SECURITIES

Generally, a business should invest any surplus cash not needed in the short-run in some type of marketable security. This investment could be for a few days, but generally is for longer periods such as 30, 60, or 90 days, or even, under certain circumstances, for up to a year.

Most businesses, particularly if their trade is seasonal, will have peaks and valleys in their cash flows and the cash surpluses from peak periods should be invested until needed during slow sales periods.

1. Risk versus liquidity

The two main factors you must consider in investing in marketable securities are risk and liquidity. A low risk investment generally yields a lower interest rate. Most government securities offer a very low risk and can generally be cashed in at any time at face value without loss of interest. However, such securities sometimes have a lower interest rate than, for example, bank term deposits or similar investments.

In certain cases a business might consider investing in the stocks and/or bonds offered by larger public companies through the various stock exchanges. The returns on these security investments can sometimes be quite high, but there is also a relatively high risk; a small business should only invest surplus cash in them with caution.

It might be a good idea to consult with your banker, or other investment advisor, to decide what is the best type of investment at any particular time for any surplus cash your business has.

f. INVENTORY

For most small businesses inventory control is critical. Inventory control requires establishing a system for ensuring that goods received are checked off against invoices, that they are stored until needed or sold, and that production or sales controls are in effect to minimize losses from inventory.

However, from an overall financial management point of view it is just as important to ensure that only the right amount of inventory is carried at any one time so that there is neither an over- nor under-investment in inventory. Inventory turnover is one way of doing this (see chapter 2).

1. Inventory turnover

Generally, the higher the turnover rate, the lower the amount of money invested in inventory, and vice versa. The inventory turnover rate can vary widely from one type of business to another, and even for businesses of the same type, although average figures for various types of business can be determined.

You should try to find out the most appropriate level of turnover for your business to avoid having too little or too much inventory. Watch for deviations from that level.

Some businesses may have several different types of inventory. For example, a manufacturing company will probably have inventories for raw materials, goods in progress, finished goods, parts, and supplies. In such cases it is a good idea to calculate inventory turnover for each type of inventory.

2. Number of days inventory

In other cases inventory turnover may not be the most appropriate measure for determining the right amount of inventory to carry. An alternative might be to value it in terms of number of days purchases or number of days sales.

For example, if inventory is worth $25,000 and represents about 25 days of sales and a "safe" level of inventory is to have only about 20 days sales on hand, inventory could be safely reduced by $5,000. This type of evaluation is useful if sales are budgeted month by month and tend to be cyclical or seasonal. Inventory can then be adjusted up or down each month in line with projected sales.

This type of inventory adjustment requires keeping a close eye on purchases and delivery times and possible delays, as well as on likely sales demand if inventory comprises a variety of different products.

Since customers generally expect you to have on hand what they want at the time they want it, you must be familiar with both the slow and the fast moving items, and which items you can purchase on short notice to keep inventory at a minimum without risk of running out.

If your business is still growing, or is planning an expansion, then you must, ahead of time, calculate the increased inventory required based on past inventory level experience. The funds for purchasing and holding this increased inventory must also be planned.

3. Economic order quantity

It costs money to hold inventory. Some of these costs are:

(a) Financing — money borrowed to purchase inventory

(b) Storage — the space built or leased to accommodate the inventory

(c) Insurance — for loss of inventory in a fire or similar event

(d) Deterioration or obsolescence — some inventory items have a limited shelf life because of style changes or spoilage, for example

(e) Breakage/damage

(f) Opportunity — an opportunity cost occurs when the money you use to purchase inventory could have been used to do something else. For example, if the money could have been left in the bank to collect interest at 10%, the opportunity cost of that money is 10%.

These various costs of holding inventory can add up to as much as 20 to 30% of the total value of that inventory. In other words, for each $1,000 of inventory the cost of holding it could range from $200 to $300 per year.

For cost reasons it is wise to use whatever means are available to you to minimize the amount you carry in inventory. One of the ways of doing this is to use the economic order quantity (EOQ) equation:

$$EOQ = \sqrt{\frac{2FS}{CP}}$$

where F = fixed cost of placing an order (bookkeeping and wage costs)

S = annual sales or usage in units of the item

C = carrying costs (as identified above)

P = purchase cost per unit.

For example, assume that a business uses about 1,000 units of an item a year, that inventory carrying costs are 15%, purchase cost per item is $12, and the fixed cost of placing an order is $8.

$$EOQ = \sqrt{\frac{2 \times \$8 \times 1{,}000}{15\% \times \$12}}$$

$$= \sqrt{\frac{\$16{,}000}{\$1.80}}$$

$$= \sqrt{8{,}888}$$

= 94 (to the nearest whole number)

Therefore, to minimize purchase and carrying costs, 94 units should be ordered each time.

g. COMPOSITION OF CURRENT ASSETS

Some current assets are more "liquid" than others, for example, cash is more liquid than accounts receivable. The more liquid the current assets are the better it is under normal circumstances. One useful method of assessing a change in current asset liquidity is to make a periodic (for example, monthly) breakdown of your current assets.

To do this, total current assets for the period are given a value of 100%, and each of the current assets is then expressed as a fraction of 100. This is illustrated as follows:

	Month 1		Month 2	
Cash	$ 45,800	28.3%	$ 70,800	40.5%
Marketable securities	30,000	18.5	4,000	2.3
Accounts receivable	46,200	28.6	50,400	28.9
Inventory	39,800	24.6	49,400	28.3
Totals	$161,800	100.0%	$174,600	100.0%

The above figures show that cash represented 28.3% of total current assets in month 1 and 40.5% in month 2. At the same time, investment in marketable securities declined from 18.5% to 2.3%. Obviously most of the marketable securities have been converted into cash. Was there a good reason for this?

The total of the most liquid current assets (cash and marketable securities) declined from 46.8% (28.3% + 18.5%) to 42.8% (40.5% + 2.3%). This would not normally be a desirable trend.

Little change occurred in accounts receivable. If a major change did take place, reference to the aging schedule for the relevant months would possibly explain the reason.

Finally, the amount in inventory increased from 24.6% to 28.3%. This is a relatively large shift and reference to the inventory turnover ratios or days sales tied up in inventory might offer an explanation.

4
CASH BUDGETING

Many small businesses make a profit according to their income statement, but don't have the cash to pay their current accounts payable. A business will not exist for long if it does not pay its bills. Cash management is therefore an extremely important part of the financial management of any small business.

Even though it is better to have too much rather than not enough cash, it is better still to have just the right amount. The objective of cash management is to determine what that correct amount is so that any surplus cash can be used to increase profits.

a. PROFIT IS NOT CASH

One of the most important facts you must remember in cash management and in analyzing income statements is that the net profit amount shown on the income statement is not the equivalent of cash. The reason for this is the accrual nature of the accounting process.

With accrual accounting, sales are recorded at the time the sale is made, even though the payment of cash for the sale might not be received until some time later.

For example, if you sell $100 worth of goods on January 15 and are paid cash at the time of the sale, the $100 will be recorded as a sale on your income statement for January and will also show as a cash receipt on your January cash flow statement.

However, if you sell $100 worth of goods on January 15 on 30-day terms and don't receive the cash until February 15, this will be recorded as a sale on your January income statement but will only show as a cash receipt on your February cash flow statement.

SAMPLE #5
BUDGETED INCOME STATEMENT

	January		February		March	
Sales		$60,000		$70,000		$80,000
Purchases	$24,000		$28,000		$32,000	
Wages	18,000		21,000		24,000	
Supplies	3,000		3,500		4,000	
Utilities	1,000		1,500		2,000	
Rent	2,000		2,000		2,000	
Advertising	1,000		1,000		1,000	
Depreciation	4,000	53,000	4,000	61,000	4,000	69,000
Net Profit		$ 7,000		$10,000		$11,000

SAMPLE #6
SALES WORKSHEET

	Month 1	Month 2	Month 3
Forecast sales			
Cash sales			
Collection of last month's charge sales			
Collection of charge sales from 2 months ago			
Collection of charge sales from more than 2 months ago			
Total cash collections			

Similarly, you can purchase supplies on credit. The goods are received and used but not paid for as long as 30 days or more. However, as long as the goods are used during the income statement period they are recorded on the income statement as an expense.

Also, some expenses may be prepaid at the beginning of the year (for example, insurance expense) yet the total insurance cost is spread equally over each monthly income statement for the entire year. For example, if in January $12,000 is paid for annual insurance, only $1,000 is recorded on the January income statement as an expense, and $1,000 will show as an expense for each of the next 11 months.

Another complicating factor is that some items, such as depreciation, are recorded as an expense on the income statements even though no cash is involved.

For these, and other reasons, the net profit shown on the income statement cannot normally be equated with cash. If you wish to equate net income with cash (a good idea in most businesses), you must convert it to a cash basis, and one of the ways to do this is to prepare cash budgets. Cash budgets are a major aid in effective cash management.

b. THE CASH BUDGET

The starting point in cash budgeting is the budgeted income statement showing the anticipated (forecast) sales and expenses by month for as long a period as is required for cash budget preparation. Without budgeted income statements it is very difficult to prepare a cash budget.

In our example we will use a three-month period. The budgeted income statements for the next three months of the business are shown in Sample #5.

In order to prepare the cash budget we need some additional information:

(a) Accounting records show that, each month, approximately 60% of the sales are in the form of cash, and 40% are on credit and collected the following month.

(b) December sales were $56,000 (you need this information to calculate the amount of cash that is going to be collected in January from sales made in December).

(c) Purchases are paid for in the month following the actual purchase. December purchases were $24,000.

(d) Wages, supplies, utilities, and rent are paid 100% by cash during each current month.

(e) Advertising has been prepaid in December ($12,000) for the entire current year. In order not to show the full $12,000 as an expense in January (since the benefit of the advertising is for a full year), the income statements show $1,000 each month for this prepaid expense.

(f) The bank balance on January 1 is $20,400.

We can now use the budgeted income statements and the above information to calculate the figures for the cash budget. The process is simple. The first cash budget month is January, and cash receipts and disbursements are calculated as follows:

1. Cash receipts

The cash receipts for April are:

(a) Current month sales $60,000 x 60% cash = $36,000

(b) Accounts receivable collections, December sales $56,000 x 40% = $22,400

In order to help you calculate and record your own cash receipts from sales you might wish to draw up a form suitable for your business similar to Sample #6.

2. Cash disbursements

The cash disbursements for April are:

(a) Purchases from December = $24,000

Again you might wish to draw up a form suitable for your business similar to Sample #7 to help you calculate and record your cash flow from purchases.

(b) Wages, 100% cash = $18,000

(c) Supplies, 100% cash = $3,000

(d) Utilities, 100% cash = $1,000
(e) Rent, 100% cash = $2,000
(f) Advertising — paid in December for the entire current year so the full $12,000 would have been recorded as a cash disbursement at that time. Therefore the cash amount for January = 0
(g) Depreciation — does not require a disbursement of cash, it is simply a write-down of the book value of the related asset(s).

3. Completed cash budget

The completed cash budget for the month of January would then be as follows:

SAMPLE #7
PURCHASES WORKSHEET

	Month 1	Month 2	Month 3
Forecast purchases			
Payments on this month's purchases			
Payments on last month's purchases			
Payments on purchases from 2 months ago			
Payments on purchases from more than 2 months ago			
Total purchases cash payments			

SAMPLE #8
CASH BUDGET

	January	February	March
Opening bank balance	$20,400	$30,800	$44,800
Receipts:			
Cash sales	36,000	42,000	48,000
Collections on accounts receivable	22,400	24,000	28,000
	$78,800	$96,800	$120,800
Disbursements:			
Purchases	$24,000	$24,000	$28,000
Wages	18,000	21,000	24,000
Supplies	3,000	3,500	4,000
Utilities	1,000	1,500	2,000
Rent	2,000	2,000	2,000
	$48,000	$52,000	$60,000
Closing bank balance	$30,800	$44,800	$60,800

January Cash Budget

Opening bank balance	$20,400
Receipts:	
Cash sales	36,000
Collections on account	22,400
Total	$78,800
Disbursements:	
Purchases	$24,000
Wages	18,000
Supplies	3,000
Utilities	1,000
Rent	2,000
Total	$48,000
Closing bank balance	$30,800

Note that the closing bank balance each month is calculated as follows:

Opening bank balance + receipts - disbursements
= closing bank balance.

Each month the closing bank balance becomes the opening bank balance of the following month.

The completed cash budget for the three-month period would be as in Sample #8. From this you can see that the bank account is expected to increase from $20,400 to $60,800 over the next three months. When the cash budget for the next quarter (April, May, and June) is prepared, it will show whether or not the bank balance is going to continue to increase or start to decline.

4. Surplus cash

From Sample #8 it is obvious that in this business there is going to be a fairly healthy surplus of cash (as long as budget projections are reasonably accurate) that should not be left to accumulate at no or low interest in a bank account. In this particular case, the owner/manager might decide to take $40,000 or $50,000 out of the bank account and invest it in high interest rate short-term (30-, 60-, or 90-day) securities.

Without preparing a cash budget, it would be difficult to know there will be surplus funds on hand that can be used to advantage to increase net profit and cash receipts. Note that if the surplus cash were taken out of the bank account and invested, the cash budget would have to show this as a disbursement until the securities were cashed in and shown as a receipt, along with the interest earned.

Similarly, interest on loans, principal payments on loans, purchases of fixed assets, income tax payments, and dividend payouts would also be recorded on the cash budget as disbursements. If any fixed assets were sold for cash the cash received would show as a receipt.

Sample #9 is a blank form that you can use as an aid in drawing up your own blank cash budget work sheet for your business. Note that it contains an extra column for each month so that actual cash flow can be compared to forecast. This refinement allows you to be more precise in cash forecasting of future months.

5. Negative cash budgets

Seasonal businesses may find that for some months of the year their disbursements exceed receipts to the point that they have negative cash budgets. Similarly, a business that is still growing, or is planning to expand, is going to need extra cash for increased inventory and to carry additional receivables until they are collected.

However, by preparing a cash budget ahead of time, the business can show that it has anticipated the cash shortage and can plan to cover it, for example by means of a short-term bank loan or line of credit. Such a loan or line of credit will be easier to obtain when the banker sees that good cash management is being practised through the preparation of a cash budget.

Any loans received to cover cash shortages will be recorded as receipts on the cash budget at that time and as disbursements when paid back.

The cash budget, particularly if prepared a year ahead, can not only help you in making decisions about investing excess funds and arranging to borrow funds to cover shortages, but also in making discretionary decisions concerning such things as major renovations, replacement of fixed assets, and payment of dividends.

c. ACCOUNTS PAYABLE

In the previous chapter, methods of managing current assets to conserve cash were discussed. However, you should not overlook your current liabilities (such as accounts payable) since cash savings can also be made there.

1. Timing of purchases and payments

Wherever possible, you should take advantage of a supplier's billing practices. Most companies supply goods as

SAMPLE #9
CASH BUDGET WORKSHEET

	MONTH 1		MONTH 2	
	FORECAST	ACTUAL	FORECAST	ACTUAL
CASH RECEIPTS				
Cash Sales				
Collections from accounts receivable ..				
Loan proceeds				
Sale of fixed assets				
Other cash received				
TOTAL CASH RECEIPTS				
CASH DISBURSEMENTS				
Payments on purchases				
Rent				
Management salaries				
Other salaries and wages				
Accounting and legal				
Utilities				
Telephone				
Repairs and maintenance				
Licenses and municipal taxes				
Insurance				
Interest				
Payments on purchase of fixed assets ..				
Payments on loans				
Income tax				
Cash dividends				
Other cash expenses				
TOTAL CASH DISBURSEMENTS				
CASH RECEIPTS LESS CASH DISBURSEMENTS				
OPENING CASH BALANCE				
CLOSING CASH BALANCE				

required during a month and within a few days of the month end mail a statement for that month to you.

Suppose you buy a month's supply of items from a supplier at the beginning of each month, using the items as required during the month and that the terms on the supplier's month end statement are 2/10, net 30. This means there is a 2% discount off the total month's purchases if the statement is paid within 10 days of the month end; otherwise the statement is payable within 30 days without discount.

You thus have the use of the supplier's credit for 40 days if you take advantage of the discount, otherwise for 60 days. In other words, you can use this "free" money to advantage, even if all you do is collect bank interest on it.

On the other hand, suppose you purchase from the same supplier, but habitually buy at the end of each month sufficient goods to carry you through until the end of the next month. In this case you will have the use of the "free" money for only 10 days, if you take advantage of the discount, and otherwise only for 30 days.

These two cases are extreme, but they do point out that wise purchasing can take advantage of a supplier's billing practices in order to increase your profits.

2. Purchase discounts

Whenever a purchase discount is offered, you should consider taking it. For example, suppose the terms are 2/10, net 60. On a $5,000 purchase paid within 10 days this would save $100 (2% x $5,000). This can amount to a considerable sum if it is made on all similar purchases made during a year.

However, in the example given, you may have to borrow the money ($4,900) in order to make the payment within 10 days. Let us assume the money is borrowed for 50 days (60 days less 10 days) at a 10% interest rate. The interest expense on this borrowed money is:

$$\frac{\$4{,}900 \times 50 \text{ days} \times 10\%}{365 \text{ days}} = \$67.12$$

In this case it would be advantageous to borrow the money since the discount saving of $100 is greater than the interest expense of $67.12.

3. Deferring payments until due

Whether you take a discount or not it is a good idea to hold on to your money (and earn interest on it) until payments are due. This does not mean delaying payments until they are delinquent since a business with a reputation for delinquency may find it has difficulty obtaining goods, supplies, and services on anything but a cash basis.

Rather it means taking advantage of a supplier's trade credit terms until the supplier expects you to pay the bill. (The use of trade credit as a form of equity financing will be discussed in more depth in chapter 7).

4. Using bank float

Another good idea for conserving cash in paying accounts is the use of bank float. A float is the difference between the bank balance shown on your records and the balance of actual cash in the bank.

This difference exists because it takes time (because of mail processing and the handling and depositing of your check by the receiver) between the moment you write a check and the moment it is deducted by your bank from your account. Since this time can be a day or two, or even longer over a weekend, you can leave that amount of surplus cash in an account bearing interest until it is needed in your current account to cover checks written and in transit.

5
EQUITY FINANCING

Regardless of its size every business needs some form of financing. In general, there are two main sources of financing: debt and equity.

With debt the lender does not have any equity or ownership in the business and thus normally no active say in the day-to-day operations of the business. Banks are one type of debt lender. Their return on the investment (loan) is the interest your business pays for the use of that money. The equity owners' return on their investment is usually in the form of withdrawals (proprietorship or partnerships) or dividends (limited company).

Before you can raise any debt financing you will normally have to show potential lenders that you are willing to invest (and risk) money in the business yourself. If you are not willing to invest in the business yourself, why should an outside lender?

a. EQUITY INVESTORS

Those who generally have an active say in the day-to-day operations of the business are the equity investors — or the owners of the company.

This equity investment could range from 10 to 50% of the total investment required. The closer to 50% it is, the easier it will be to borrow and the higher your profits might be (since you will have less interest expense on borrowed money that will eat into those profits).

However, the higher the equity, the lower might be your actual return on investment since you are reducing the opportunity to trade on the lender's investment. This is known as using leverage (see chapter 2).

1. Personal funds

The most common source of equity capital is personal funds from savings. Over the past few years many entrepreneurs have been able to provide this initial equity because of inflation. Inflation has caused home values to increase to the point that they could be remortgaged to provide a form of instant cash.

2. Friends or relatives

The equity investment could be further increased from the savings of friends willing to invest, or even from relatives (love money). However, many otherwise successful small businesses have created problems by bringing in friends and/or relatives as investors.

Mixing social or family relationships with business is always risky, particularly if the business is not doing as well as everyone initially imagined, or if the terms and conditions of such loans are not clearly spelled out to prevent these lenders insisting on becoming involved in day-to-day matters. Also, if a relative dies, the heirs may immediately demand their money back, with interest, under the threat of a lawsuit.

To avoid these problems make sure any friend or family loans are covered by written agreements, preferably drawn up by a lawyer. In this way agreements will at least be viewed by those lenders on a businesslike basis. Agreement should be reached on such matters as:

(a) Rate of interest to be paid
(b) When the loans will be retired (paid back), and any option to pay them back early
(c) The procedures that all parties will follow if loans become delinquent

3. Employees

Your employees can be another source of internal equity financing. Employees who have savings may be interested in investing them in your company since they understand its products and know and trust its owners. They also feel they are in an advantageous position to closely monitor their investment.

An employee with an investment in a company is also likely to feel more motivated and be concerned about the company's success. The main disadvantage is that it may be difficult to fire or retire an unproductive or uncooperative employee who has an equity investment in your business.

4. Loans versus shares

If your business is an incorporated one, the equity investment could be in the form of stockholder loans, or common stock or shares (to be discussed in the next section), or a combination of loans and shares. How the owners' or equity investors' investment in the company is structured will vary in each different situation.

However, generally speaking, the advantage of money invested as loans is that it can easily be paid back to lenders without tax, other than personal tax on any interest the lender receives from the company before all the loan is finally paid off.

If the money is in the form of shares, it may be more difficult to get your money back since shares must be sold to someone else or back to the company.

On the other hand, banks and other debt investors are skeptical of shareholder loans because of the ease with which they can be repaid, and because it would be feasible for you to borrow money from a debt lender and use the cash to pay yourself back your own loan investment.

The outside debt investors may therefore place restrictions or conditions on when and how the company can pay off shareholder loans, redeem shares, or possibly even pay dividends on shares. These restrictions or conditions are imposed to protect the debt investors.

You should seek the advice of a tax accountant since your personal tax situation and that of other equity investors and the degree of financial success of the business, can have a bearing on whether the shareholders' investment should be in the form of loans or shares.

b. SHARES

Unless your company is a proprietorship or partnership it will have issued some shares. In a one-person company those shares will be held by the owner. A larger company may possibly have several owners or shareholders.

A small company can often raise more equity capital by issuing more shares, for cash, to all its present shareholders who operate the company. It can make financial decisions with little or no formality.

As a business grows larger and operating procedures become more formal shares may be issued to new shareholders. Major financial decisions must be discussed and approved by the board of directors whose responsibility it is to run the company.

1. Common shares

In most cases the shareholders of smaller companies will own common shares with each share entitling its owner to one vote at shareholder meetings. In closely held companies, where the original owner or owners want to retain full voting power the voting rights might be limited to a particular class of common shares, and all or most of those shares will be held by the few who wish to retain complete control of, and be responsible for, the company's operations.

Alternatively, different classes of common shares may have equal voting rights, but the quantities issued and the selling prices of each class are arranged so that effective control is still in the hands of those who wish to control the business.

For example, consider the situation of a new company that issues both class A and class B common shares to raise $100,000 of equity capital. Each share of either class carries one vote. Class A shares will be sold for $1 and 80,000 will be issued — total $80,000. Class B shares will be sold for 10¢ and 200,000 will be issued — total $20,000. Thus the B shareholders have effective voting control since they own 2½ times as many shares (200,000 versus 80,000) and yet have put up only 20% of the total equity capital.

Of course, in order to sell the class A shares in this particular way the class B shareholders generally have to give up something such as receiving a lower dividend rate, or no dividends until retained earnings have reached a minimum stipulated level.

The class B shareholders might be quite happy to give up something since they control such matters as future methods of financing, whether or not any dividends will be paid, the form that further common share issues will take including selling prices and voting rights, and similar matters.

2. Advantages of common shares

The major advantage of common share financing is that the shareholders control the company and benefit the most if the company is successful.

Also, with common shares the company is not committed to pay dividends although you would normally expect dividends to be paid if the business is successful.

If the business is successful, the value of its common shares increases and its ability to obtain short, intermediate, and long-term financing (with its advantage of leverage) increases.

In times of inflation the ownership of common shares provides protection even if only against inflation because the assets (such as land and building) usually increase in value. There is also the potential for capital gain on the sale of the shares if the company is taken over by another.

Other advantages of common share financing are that it —

(a) is an easier and faster way to raise money,
(b) expands the borrowing power of the business,
(c) reduces the risk to each of the business's shareholders,
(d) improves the credit rating with suppliers, and
(e) adds the experience and advice of new shareholders to the company.

3. Disadvantages of common shares

The major disadvantage of common share financing is that since common shares are equity and represent ownership of the company, but only after all other liabilities are paid off, common shareholders are therefore the first to suffer if the company is unsuccessful.

Another disadvantage of common shares, particularly to the original investors, is that voting control may be diluted as more shares are issued and more shareholders are involved, although this can be overcome, as illustrated earlier, using nonvoting classes of common shares. Also, dividends to common shareholders are not tax deductible to the company as is interest on debt financing.

Other disadvantages are:

(a) It may reduce the flexibility of the company since there are more shareholders to contend with.

(b) It increases costs to the company from issuing additional shares, making dividend payments, and increasing accounting controls and legal and accounting costs, as well as brokerage costs if the company is a public one.

c. PREFERRED SHARES

Common shares are not the only method of equity financing for an incorporated company. Preferred shares can also be issued. Preferred shares usually have priority, with reference to dividends and assets, over common shares. Dividend priority is usually limited to a dividend rate stated as a fixed percentage of the par, or face, value of the preferred shares.

However, to the company, payment of dividends is not a legal obligation as is the payment of interest on a mortgage. In other words, the company will only pay dividends on preferred shares if it has the money to do so.

1. Cumulative preferred

To protect the preferred shareholders in such situations, preferred shares are usually cumulative. This means if the dividend is not paid, it accumulates and must eventually be paid before any dividends can be paid to the holders of common shares.

2. Classes of preferred

Various classes of preferred shares can also be issued carrying different voting rights. These voting rights can be full (on an equal basis, share for share, with common stock), nonvoting, or limited voting. With limited voting preferred shareholders might obtain full voting rights if the company does not pay its preferred share dividends.

3. Redeemable preferred

Redeemable preferred shares may be issued. The redeemable feature allows your company the option to buy back those preferred shares at a stipulated price usually at or above the preferred shares' face or par value. By issuing redeemable preferred shares, a company, when it has the cash, can cancel any inhibiting, restrictive covenants (see below) that the preferred shares placed on common stock owners.

4. Convertible preferred

As an alternative to redeemable preferred stock, shares may be made convertible at the preferred shareholders' choice. In other words, the preferred shareholder, when the time is right, has the option to convert the preferred into a stipulated number of common shares.

5. Advantages of preferred

Since preferred shares are a form of equity financing, the selling of preferred shares to raise money broadens the equity base and could make future debt financing easier since it reduces the debt to equity ratio.

Also, even though preferred shares may carry a stipulated dividend rate that may also be cumulative, those dividends, unlike interest on a mortgage, do not have to be paid on a specified date if the company is currently short of cash.

Finally, issuing preferred shares is a method of using equity financing without losing or diluting voting control as long as dividends can be paid.

6. Disadvantages of preferred

A major disadvantage of preferred share financing is that dividends are not deductible by the company for income tax purposes. Consider the situation of a company that requires $100,000 for expansion and expects to earn, before interest and income taxes, $18,000 on this additional investment. The company is in a 50% tax bracket and can obtain the $100,000 either by a 15% loan or by issuing 15% preferred shares. The following shows the net profit remaining for common shareholders under either alternative. In this situation, preferred shares are a disadvantage.

	Loan financing	Preferred share financing
Income before interest and tax	$18,000	$18,000
Interest 15% x $100,000	15,000	
Profit before income tax	$ 3,000	$18,000
Income tax 50%	1,500	9,000
Profit before dividends	$ 1,500	$ 9,000
Preferred share dividends		15,000
Net profit (loss)	$ 1,500	($ 6,000)

However, despite the above, financial decisions must also consider the effect of a proposed financing arrangement on potential investors. It may be easier to raise money from preferred shares than from a loan. Investors may be attracted to the preferred shares because of a participating dividend or from being able to sell back their preferred shares to the company at a profit, or by being able to eventually convert them into common shares.

7. Restrictions

Preferred stock may restrict the actions of common shareholders. For example, this can be done by restricting the issuing of further preferred shares ranking equally or ahead of issued preferred without those shareholders' approval.

There may be other restrictions such as the amount or type of further debt that may be assumed, or a limit on the payment of dividends on common shares to profits generated subsequent to the issuing of the preferred shares and then only if working capital is above a certain specified amount.

d. DIVIDEND POLICY

A dividend policy is necessary for any company that has shareholders. This policy is necessary so that the company's profits can be effectively divided between reinvestment in the company for its continued growth or expansion, or payment of dividends to the shareholders.

Shareholders expect dividends (since that is often the reason they purchased shares in the first place), but if the company's objective is growth this may necessitate the retention of some, if not all, of the profits or retained earnings of the business.

In such a case the objectives of company growth and dividend payments are in conflict and the company's dividend policy is therefore a critical financial decision in all but one-person companies.

Dividends can only be paid from current or previous years' retained earnings. Further, in order to protect the creditors, the law prohibits a company paying dividends if liabilities exceed assets (in other words, if the company is insolvent).

Even if assets exceed liabilities, a company must have cash available to pay dividends and, as you know from chapter 4, a profit does not necessarily mean that cash is available.

Sometimes dividend restrictions are imposed by lenders. For example, a bank debt lender may require that a minimum working capital level must be maintained before dividends that would impair working capital can be paid. Also, if preferred shares have been issued, dividends usually have to be paid on those preferred shares before common stock dividends can be paid.

A company that is expanding rapidly will generally use most of its accumulated profits for expansion, leaving less for dividends. A company with relatively stable and predictable earnings will usually pay out more of its earnings, on a percentage basis, than a company whose earnings are cyclical or difficult to predict.

e. GOING PUBLIC

Small and closely held companies do not face the dilemma of whether or not to go public. However, as a company grows, even without wide common share ownership, it can end up going public as a result of shareholders selling off their shares to "outsiders."

However, the procedure of going public formally in order to sell the shares widely requires the company to conform to the laws concerning the sale of securities. Any company wishing to go public this way must follow the required procedures.

If a company's shares are traded through brokers, but not through an organized stock exchange, it is referred to as "over the counter." Once a company has grown sufficiently, particularly in number of shareholders and public acceptance and marketability of its shares, you may wish to consider a formal listing with a stock exchange, although such a listing by itself does not guarantee an active trading of the shares.

1. Disadvantages

There are disadvantages to an exchange listing. For example, more public attention is focused on companies that are listed. Also, if the value of the company's shares declines in difficult times, speculators may be attracted and a takeover or merger may become possible and control lost by the original company developers. The likelihood of speculative manipulation of the shares may also be increased causing wide pricing fluctuations.

Finally, when shares are publicly traded, management frequently becomes concerned with what is happening to the price of the shares rather than making sound, long-run business decisions.

The decision to go public is a serious one. Raising funds through a new issue of shares to the public is a long, arduous, and precarious process requiring good timing. It can take from three to six months and cost anywhere from $25,000 to $100,000. It should, therefore, not even be contemplated unless you require a very large amount of money — say, at least $500,000.

In order to arrange a sale of shares to the public, you will need an investment dealer or financial middleman with the expertise to bring together a company that requires capital with those who have money to invest.

2. Selling shares to a larger company

One other possibility is to sell shares to a larger company. Larger companies are sometimes quite interested in investing in smaller companies without taking over control.

Their motivation is the desire to become involved with an individual or small company in an unfamiliar business field with the intention of expanding into it in a major way at some later date.

Alternatively, the operations of the large and small companies may be complementary to each other.

In any such situation you would be well advised to seek the help of your accountant, lawyer, and other professional advisors very early in the discussions.

6
DEBT FINANCING

In this chapter we will take a look at two matters related to debt financing: interest rates and security. In the following chapters we will cover the various types of debt financing available and the sources of financing.

a. INTEREST

Banks and other financial institutions vary interest rates according to money market conditions. The rates can change frequently.

Lending institutions use money from various sources to make their loans. The amount of interest that the lender is paying to use those funds and the length of the loan determine the interest that the lender will charge you.

Rates also vary depending on the customer. The prime rate is generally the lowest rate available. Rates increase above that depending on the specific business, its credit rating, its size, and other factors. It would not be unreasonable (because of the risk involved to the lender) to suggest that most small businesses in need of bank credit probably pay rates that tend to be among the highest.

1. Short-term loans

Interest on short-term loans reflects the interest rate currently paid by the lender on short-term deposits such as savings accounts. The interest paid on savings accounts depends on money market conditions or the supply and demand for short-term funds. International borders are not necessarily ignored in the equation since those with funds to deposit in banks will often seek out the most favorable rates, regardless of country.

The best indicator of short-term interest rates of various kinds is the prime rate — the lowest rate that an individual lender charges to its largest and most creditworthy customers.

Small businesses are usually not large enough to be considered candidates for the prime rate, but by keeping an eye on the daily quote fluctuations in the prime rate the small business borrower can have a good idea how much above the prime rate must be paid to obtain short-term funds.

2. Long-term loans

Lenders who have pools of funds available from depositors who have left money with them for a minimum of at least a year, and preferably longer, may be able to lend money for longer terms and at lower rates than those charged on short-term loans.

However, in volatile money markets where interest rates are unpredictable long-term lending rates, since they are sometimes fixed and not subject to change during the term of the loan, can be higher than current short-term rates.

Because of this situation, and the fact that lenders have been hurt in volatile money markets, you may be unable to find a fixed interest rate on a long-term loan.

These long-term loans are subject to two or three-year terms and balloon payments. A balloon payment means that at the end of the term the balance of the loan is technically due and payable. However, in practice the lender can renegotiate the loan (generally in the lender's favor) at that time, adjusting the interest rate and other terms.

Variable rate long-term loans are also becoming more common. A variable rate long-term loan simply means that the interest rates are adjustable, at the discretion of the lender, as frequently as monthly. The rate may go up or down depending on money market conditions. These market conditions take into consideration the current inflation rate and the market's expectation of the future inflation rate.

3. Interest spread

Borrowers frequently ask why the rate paid on savings accounts or other bank deposits is less, sometimes as much as three or four points, than the amount charged on loans.

The reason is that the bank has its expenses, just as your business has, for operating costs (such as interest paid on deposits, rent, wages, supplies) and overhead expenses (such as management salaries, building rent, insurance) and must itself have a difference between the total of those costs and the income it receives in interest and service charges received. In other words, the lender must make a profit and a reasonable return on investment.

In addition, just as you may make sales to individuals or companies who are unable to pay their accounts, so too the lender must "absorb" losses on loans made to individuals or companies who are unable to pay.

These losses are not in fact absorbed by the lender any more than the losses you sustain in your business are absorbed by you. They are built into the selling price you charge for goods and services, and a money lender builds them into the selling price, i.e., into the interest rate charged.

However, since bankers, just like you, are in competition with other lenders or other businesses, their interest rates are competitive, just as your prices have to be. This means that, in seeking a loan, you should search out the lender with the most favorable lending rate and conditions, just as you would expect astute customers to seek you out if you offered the best quality at a competitive price.

Generally, however you will find that the larger the amount you wish to borrow, the longer the period of the loan, and the greater the risk the lender considers it to be, the higher the interest rate. The more stable the company, the longer it has been in business, the larger it is, and similar factors tend to reduce the risk and therefore the interest rate to the borrower.

b. SECURITY

Most lenders require some sort of security for loans made to small businesses. For intermediate- and long-term loans this security is quite specific and will be discussed in chapter 8. For short-term loans of a year or less this security will probably take the form of one or more of the following.

1. Personal guarantees

Even if your business is incorporated, the lender may require your personal guarantee or endorsement of the loan in the event your company does not meet its debt obligations. This means that if your company defaults on its repayments, the lender can claim against your personal assets such as your savings, your home, and your car.

If your case for a loan is not a strong one, you will normally have little choice but to provide this personal guarantee or endorsement. If there are other partners or shareholders in the company, they might also be required to sign guarantees.

In some cases, where neither you nor other principals in the company can provide sufficient security to the lender you may be asked to find an outside guarantor. If your case is so weak that you need an outside guarantor, you might question whether or not you should really be making the loan in the first place.

A guarantee may be limited or unlimited. A limited guarantee gives the lender the right to demand that you repay, on request, the amount owing on that specific loan. An unlimited guarantee gives the lender the right to demand that you repay, on request, all loans due to that lender. Obviously it is preferable for you to have a limited guarantee.

Make sure that when any guaranteed loan is paid off you obtain a release from the guarantee. If a personal guarantee is required by the lender in addition to other security, try to negotiate a guarantee only for the amount of the shortfall and not for the full amount of the loan.

Also, if you have made your own direct loan to your company and were obliged by the debt lender to sign a postponement of claim for your own loan, make sure that the postponement of claim is cancelled after the debt lender is paid off.

Similarly, if during the period of the debt, restrictions were placed on payment of dividends to you, or if life insurance policies were assigned to the lender, have these restrictions removed and/or the policies changed to revert to you.

It may be that your company has made loans to you or other principals in the company. If so the lender may require you and the others to subordinate your claims to the claims of the lender by signing an appropriate subordination agreement.

2. Assignment of lease

You may be in the business of leasing out assets in which case the security for the lender may be an assigned lease or leases.

An assigned lease is similar to a guarantee. The bank or other institution lends the money on the security of a leased asset and is assigned the lease and the lender (instead of you) automatically receives the rent payments which go toward reducing the loan.

3. Warehouse receipt

Lenders sometimes require a warehouse receipt as security for a loan. This receipt is delivered to the lender and shows that the commodity or product used as security is either in a public warehouse or on your premises. The warehouse receipt is for a percentage of the estimated value of the items used as security, and these items normally have to be readily marketable.

4. Savings accounts

You may be able to obtain a loan, all else failing, by assigning your personal savings account to the lender as security.

While it is assigned your withdrawals from it will be limited.

5. Life insurance

Instead of raising cash from your insurance company based on your policy's paid up cash value, you may be able to raise the cash by assigning your policy instead to a bank since it may be easier and speedier to obtain the cash that way.

6. Stocks and bonds

If you have marketable stocks and bonds, you may be able to use them as security or collateral for a loan. These have to be gilt edged stocks, and the maximum you can expect might be up to 75% of their market value.

Alternatively, if you have government bonds, it might go as high as 90%. If the market value on your stocks and/or bonds drops while they are secured, you may have to put up additional security or reduce the loan.

7

SHORT-TERM FINANCING

Short-term financing is generally considered to be funding required for a period of less than a year. In short-term financing the lender will tend to place greater emphasis on your balance sheet in order to see if, in case of your business's liquidation, current assets would provide sufficient funds to repay the debt.

This differs from intermediate- and long-term financing (to be discussed in the next chapter) where lenders rely more on the earning power of your company and its ability to repay longer loans out of ongoing profits.

One basic rule of finance is that short-term requirements for cash should be provided by short-term financing, and longer-term requirements by intermediate- or long-term financing.

If this rule is not followed, you might end up with a financing imbalance. For example, this could happen if you made a short-term one-year bank loan and used the money to buy long-life equipment. If that happened, you might find yourself short of cash to purchase inventory, carry receivables, pay your payables, and even short of cash to pay back the one-year loan! You could even be forced into liquidation or bankruptcy in such a situation.

a. INTERNAL FINANCING

One method of raising short-term funding is by internal financing.

Internal financing is sometimes referred to as bootstrap financing. This means using your company's ability to generate cash or capital from profits and thus reduce the need for equity and debt financing.

Earlier, some of the ways to generate internal cash through effective working capital management were discussed. When you can indicate to a lender that you are practicing good working capital management and maximizing the use of internal funds you will be more likely to find external short-term financing on reasonable terms when you need it.

b. TRADE CREDIT

Surprisingly the most common means of short-term financing is trade credit or financial assistance from companies you buy from. The reason for this is that most suppliers do not demand cash on delivery (COD) other than in those cases where a business has a reputation for delinquency in payment of accounts.

Usually a bill or invoice for purchases is sent at the month end. In the case of, let us say, a 30-day payment period for items purchased at the beginning of a month this would mean that you use the service or supplies received without cost for anywhere up to 60 days.

To a small business this type of trade credit is an important source of cash. Even if you had the cash to pay the bill at the time it was received it may not be wise to do so.

As long as there is no penalty imposed you are free to let your cash sit in the bank and collect interest until the invoice has to be paid. To you this is another source of profit.

1. Open credit

This type of trade credit is sometimes called "open credit" since it is generally arranged on an understanding between buyer and seller without any formal agreement documented in writing.

One type of open credit arrangement is for the supplier to extend credit for a specific number of days after delivery of the goods, or after the month end following delivery of the goods, with no cash discount permitted. In other words, the full amount of the invoice or invoices must be paid.

Another arrangement is for the supplier to offer both a credit period and a cash discount. One common discount type is referred to as 2/10, net 30. This means that you are offered a 2% discount off the invoice price if the bill is paid within 10 days. If the bill is not paid within the 10-day period, it must be paid within a further 20 days but without discount. This type of arrangement is made to encourage you to pay bills promptly (purchase discounts were discussed in chapter 4).

Another type of trade credit is to obtain goods on consignment. This is common in certain types of business. When you receive goods on consignment the supplier retains ownership of them. You only pay the supplier when the goods are sold.

2. Establishing credit

If your business is relatively new and on COD with suppliers, you may initially have to borrow to pay those suppliers in order to establish and maintain good supplier relations and build up a solid credit base.

You should also be ready to provide a supplier with prompt credit references when asked in order to help establish your trade credit. Most larger suppliers will have credit departments, or will employ an agency, to check on your credit status if you are a new customer desiring trade credit.

When you have established a good credit standing with a supplier you should pay your bills on time, otherwise you might find yourself being reverted to a COD basis. Maintaining a good credit record with a supplier may mean that one day your supplier might be interested in investing money in your business if you are expanding.

As you build up your credit record with suppliers you might later be able to negotiate more favorable trade credit terms, such as extending the time period before payment is required or receiving a larger discount on invoices paid promptly.

However, don't become too attached to one or two suppliers simply because they provide liberal trade credit terms. You might find you are locked into a situation when a supplier's prices no longer remain competitive in price, quality, delivery, or service.

In the discussion so far it is assumed that you pay bills by the end of the supplier's payment period. If you delay paying beyond that date, you are using this "free" money at a further cost to the supplier.

For this reason, suppliers do not encourage the practice. Banks and other lending institutions also look unfavorably on businesses that make a habit of not paying bills promptly.

If you have this reputation, you might well find that suppliers will deliver only on a COD basis. You might also find it difficult to borrow funds when needed for short-term purposes.

3. Special situations

However, if the nature of your business is seasonal, you might find it difficult to pay all bills in the off season when they are due. In such cases it might be wise to arrange for a longer payment period with suppliers whose financial resources allow them to extend longer credit.

Alternatively, arrangements could be made with a lending institution to borrow funds for the interim period so that bills can be paid within the normal payment period.

Keep suppliers, particularly major ones, advised in advance if you are going to have to defer payment of their account for some reason. Alerting suppliers this way might prevent ill will and credit curtailment if, for example, your business is suffering a slight downturn in difficult economic times.

Don't forget that in difficult economic conditions the supplier might also be forced into curtailing trade credit. In other words, trade credit is not a right that you have in perpetuity.

Finally you should also recognize that trade credit is not absolutely free. The supplier who extends credit also has financing costs, which must be paid out of revenue from the products sold. In other words, the cost is included in the selling prices. Where competition exists among suppliers, however, this hidden cost should be minimized.

c. SHORT-TERM OR OPERATING LOANS

Short-term or operating loans (sometimes referred to as commercial loans) are for financing inventory, accounts receivable, special purchases, prepaid promotions, and other items requiring working capital during peak periods. Normally an amount up to 10% of annual sales can be borrowed to finance such requirements.

These loans are considered to be self-liquidating since they are paid back when the inventory or receivables financed by them are converted to cash that is then used to pay off the loan.

The main sources of short-term loans are commercial banks or similar financing institutions. Using a short-term loan is a good way to establish credit with a bank. When such a lender considers a short-term loan it will be very interested in your business's liquidity. If you have a healthy working capital, collect your accounts receivable promptly and have a rapid rate of inventory turnover, your business will be a good prospect for a short-term loan.

1. Security required

This type of loan could be secured or unsecured. If secured, the security might be any or all of the following:

(a) A fixed or floating charge debenture on accounts receivable, inventory, equipment, or fixtures. The lender can register this debenture in a similar way to a mortgage on land and building.

(b) A general assignment of your accounts receivable. You collect the receivables in the normal way unless you are in default of the loan. In that case the lender assumes collection of the receivables. When receivables are assigned you normally have to submit to the lender a list of the outstanding ones each month.

(c) An assignment of fire insurance and, in some cases, key employee or personal life insurance policies

(d) Stocks or bonds that you or your company owns

(e) A personal guarantee by you and/or your spouse (when personal assets are registered in the spouse's name)

2. Terms

Short-term loans are usually negotiated for specific periods of time (for example 30, 60, or 90 days, and less frequently for periods up to a year or more) and may be repayable in a lump sum at the end of the period, or in periodic installments.

If you have adequate collateral, short-term loans of up to a year can sometimes be negotiated.

Each separate borrowing is usually covered by a promissory note (a form of contract spelling out the interest rate and terms of the loan), and the interest rate is frequently subject to change, particularly in erratic money markets.

3. Interest rate

The interest rate is usually a stated annual interest rate. The stated rate may differ from the effective (or true) rate if the loan is discounted. Discounting means that the interest on the loan is deducted in advance.

If a $1,000 bank loan is taken out at the beginning of the year, to be repaid at the end of the year at a discount (interest) rate of 15%, you would receive $850 ($1,000, less 15% of $1,000, or $150), and repay $1,000 at the end of the year. Since you have only $850, the effective interest rate is

$$\frac{\$150}{\$850} \times 100 = 17.6\%$$

The effective interest rate also differs from the stated rate if a loan is repayable in equal installments over the term of the loan, rather than in a lump sum at the end of the loan period as in the case above.

Consider a $1,200 loan at a 12% rate, repayable in equal monthly installments of principal over a year ($100 per month) plus interest. If the interest is calculated on the initial loan, it will be 12% of $1,200, or $144 ($12 per month).

The effective rate of interest will be higher than the stated 12% since you do not have the use of the full $1,200 for the year.

Tables are available from most bookstores or stationery retailers from which an exact rate of interest can be determined under various circumstances, but an approximate effective rate of interest can be quickly calculated.

With equal monthly repayments, on average the borrower has only half the $1,200 for use over the year, or $600 ($1,200 divided by 2). The effective interest rate is then

$$\frac{\$144}{\$600} \times 100 = 24\%$$

which is double the stated rate.

In all cases where money is being borrowed, and particularly where you are shopping around for the best rate, it is important to know what the effective interest rate is.

d. LINE OF CREDIT

A line of credit is an agreement between you and a bank, or similar financial institution, specifying the maximum amount of credit (overdraft) the bank will allow you at any one time.

Credit lines are usually established for one-year periods, subject to annual renegotiation and renewal, with the bank taking your accounts receivable and inventory as security.

Generally, accounts receivable, as long as they are not overdue, may be financed up to 75% and inventory up to 50%. A line of credit is useful for a seasonal business with a need to carry considerably more inventory and at the same time carry a much larger than normal accounts receivable from charge sales that create a peak season financial need.

The amount of credit is based on the bank's assessment of the creditworthiness of the company and its credit requirements. This type of loan is sometimes called a demand loan since the bank can demand that it be repaid immediately without notice. However, this would not happen under normal circumstances.

If you are a borrower whose company has a record of profitability, you may qualify for an unsecured line of credit. Banks generally extend a line of credit for one year. However, an unsecured line of credit is usually revolving; in other words, you can repeatedly borrow, repay, and borrow again all or part of the credit available.

In order to secure a line of credit you may have to sign short-term notes to evidence the advances. These notes are periodically reviewed and repaid, reduced, or extended, as required.

The establishment of a line of credit protects you since normally the lender will not reduce or cancel the line of credit without good cause. However, the lender will keep an eye on your financial statements and economic and other factors that might influence your business's operations and thus change the lender's view of the appropriateness of your particular line of credit.

With a line of credit you only pay interest on money actually borrowed — not on the amount that could be. This interest may be supplemented by a small commitment fee of less than 1% on any unused portion of the line of credit.

1. Compensating balance

A business with a line of credit of any sizable amount (generally $100,000 or more) is sometimes required to keep a deposit balance with the lender. This deposit balance is usually proportional to the amount of the line of credit.

For example, it might be stipulated by the lender at 10% to 15% of the line of credit amount. This percentage might vary with the money market. Since the deposit amount is generally in an account that pays little or no interest it favors the bank and increases the effective interest rate you are paying on any money used from your line of credit.

Some banks charge service fees or ask for a higher interest rate in lieu of a compensating balance.

e. ASSIGNING ACCOUNTS RECEIVABLE

Most small businesses need cash to meet their current liability commitments, and if money is tied up in receivables a cash problem can arise. This problem is particularly so in a growing business with expanding sales.

In such a situation receivables tend to increase at the expense of cash, inventories, and even fixed assets. Unless receivables can be converted into cash in a minimum period of time the business's liquidity may be impaired. It may then run into credit problems and find its growth limited.

Attention should be paid to control of accounts receivable and collection procedures. These controls and procedures were outlined in chapter 3. In addition you might want to consider financing your accounts receivable.

Receivables can be assigned to a bank or other lender as security for a short-term loan or line of credit. The receivables can be assigned on a notification or nonnotification basis. Under a notification basis the lender notifies your customers that the accounts receivable have been pledged to the lender and directs them to make payment directly to the lender. Since this arrangement can disturb the normal relationship between you and your customers a nonnotification basis is more common.

Under nonnotification customers continue to make payment to you. In other words you collect the receivables in the normal way, even though they are assigned. You will sign a note to the lender, and as the receivables are collected by you you pay back the lender and retrieve your note.

Generally the lender will loan up to a certain percentage of the face value of the assigned receivables (for example, 65%) and charge you interest and possibly a service fee.

If collections on assigned accounts are not sufficient to pay the loan, you will be responsible for the deficiency. This is a major difference from factoring. Under factoring the lender purchases your accounts receivable and takes over the loss from any uncollectible accounts (bad debts).

With accounts receivable financing you are able to secure a continuous source of operating cash without having to make long-term financing agreements. The receivables line is usually arranged for a year and renewed at the end of that time if agreed to by the lender.

The main aim of accounts receivable financing is to free up funds tied up in this asset. This may put your company in a stronger position to expand sales, provide cash to pay off accounts payable to receive a discount, and improve your credit standing.

However, accounts receivable financing is not the answer to a permanent working capital deficiency but is more usefully used to cover cyclical or seasonal shortages of cash to cover current obligations as they fall due.

f. INVENTORY FINANCING

Some small businesses may have large amounts of money tied up in inventory of raw materials, work in process, or in finished goods. The cost of carrying this inventory can be as high as 30% of its value, therefore you might want to consider inventory financing.

Inventories are not as liquid as accounts receivable, so a bank or other lender will normally want to secure any loans made for inventory only after you have used your full ability to borrow against accounts receivable. Receivables are easier to convert into cash in the short run and do not present the same problems that certain inventories can create such as style changes, sharp price reductions, or obsolescence.

Retail and similar businesses that must carry large amounts of unsold inventory will probably experience difficulty, particularly in a new business, in obtaining inventory financing. The reason is that such businesses can have a high failure rate and lenders are not anxious to accept certain types of merchandise (that they would later have difficulty disposing of if the loan were in default) as security.

In those cases, to be financible, the inventory must have a ready market and not subject to obsolescence or perishable in any way. In other words, the inventory has to be able to be sold if you cannot meet your loan payments.

In a manufacturing or processing situation only raw material and finished goods inventory could be financed. A lender would not wish to finance work in process since it has virtually no resale value.

Despite these difficulties, inventory financing can be quite important to your business, particularly if you must build up inventory to meet a seasonal demand for your products.

The marketability of your inventory will dictate the percentage of its value that can be financed. If it is not readily marketable, this percentage could be as low as 30% to 40%. If it is extremely marketable it could be as high as 70% or 80%. The lender will probably require a warehouse receipt or trust receipt for the inventory.

g. OTHER LOANS

Some other types of loan are:

1. Collateral loan

You may be able to obtain a bank loan on the basis of collateral such as a chattel mortgage, stocks and bonds, cash surrender value of life insurance, and similar security.

Even with this collateral, regardless of how good it is, the lender may feel that it is no guarantee of your business's ability to repay because the lender's objective is not to cash in the collateral (since it may produce less in liquidation than the amount you owe).

However, the collateral does afford the lender some security, and a collateral loan may be easier to find than a line of credit or unsecured loan for a risky business.

2. Character loan

A character loan is a short-term unsecured loan, generally restricted to an individual or his or her company with an excellent credit rating.

3. Warehouse receipt loan

If goods are stored in a warehouse, and warehouse receipts are used as security for a loan, the loan may then be used to pay off the supplier. As you sell the goods the loan is paid off.

4. Floor plan financing

Floor planning is used as a financing vehicle by retailers of large ticket items (automobiles, appliances) that can be readily identified, usually by a serial number, and have a relatively high unit value.

In floor planning you have possession of the units and the lender retains the ownership and pays the manufacturer the cost price of the items. As you sell each item you pay the lender the amount due on that item.

You will generally sign a note to the lender and pay interest from the time the arrangement is made until the time the item is sold. A flooring line might be renewed annually.

A trust receipt is frequently used as a legal document in floor plan financing. It acknowledges that you have received the items being floor planned, that you agree to keep them in trust for the lender, and that you promise to pay back the lender as you sell items.

5. Indirect collection financing

Indirect collection financing is also used for big ticket items sold by you to your customers on an installment paying basis. The lender will advance you 70% to 80% of the value of each item when it is sold to a customer. You repay the advance with interest as the customer pays you each installment.

6. Chattel mortgage

A chattel mortgage loan is usually for a short- or intermediate-term. It is secured by the movable assets (chattels) of your business that are not otherwise mortgaged or secured. The chattel mortgage provides a lien to the lender. To obtain the mortgage for your business you might have to include personal assets in the security.

The value assigned to the assets is their current liquidation value. You may be required to carry various types of insurance on the mortgaged chattels. The security is released or discharged to you when the loan is repaid.

7. Floating charge debenture

A floating charge debenture is again a short- or intermediate-term loan where the loan is secured by a general claim on the total equity of the business.

A floating charge debenture (unlike a chattel mortgage or a commercial pledge that specifies and describes specific assets as security) does not describe specific assets. Instead, all the assets are described in general terms (for example, "inventory") and can be disposed of in the ordinary day-to-day operations of the business unless loan default occurs.

As a precaution the lender may impose certain restrictions or controls to ensure that your business's equity does not fall below what the lender deems is required to secure the loan.

A business with a floating charge debenture may still be able to obtain other short-term financing on specific assets, for example through a chattel mortgage.

The lender holding a floating charge debenture ranks after the claims of other lenders whose claims are on specific assets.

8

INTERMEDIATE- AND LONG-TERM FINANCING

Most financing that is for more than one year is referred to as long-term. However, somewhere between short- and long-term financing is a need at times for intermediate-term financing for periods up to five years. Long-term financing is generally for periods from 5 to 25 years.

a. INTERMEDIATE-TERM FINANCING

When considering an intermediate-term loan lending companies rely on indications of your business's profitability and ability to repay. These indications are provided by income statement and cash flow forecasts for the next several years, as well as historic income statements that indicate your forecasts are reasonable and not made on the basis of overestimated sales and underestimated expenses.

A common way to obtain this intermediate-term financing is through term loans.

1. Term loans

Term loans are usually obtained from banks or similar financial institutions and are usually arranged to cover the purchase of basic inventory, leasehold improvements, and assets such as furniture, fixtures, and equipment. Generally 60% to 75% of the cost of these items can be obtained through term loans.

Term loans are usually repaid in regular installments of principal and interest over the life of the loan, which is usually less than the life of the assets for which financing is required. Term loans could vary in length from one to five years.

The interest rate on term loans is usually a percentage point or more higher than that for a short-term loan made to the same borrower.

The periodic payments on term loans can be geared to the business's cash flow ability to repay. In some cases only the interest portion of such loans is payable in the first year or two. Payments could be monthly, quarterly, semiannually, or annually. Payments are calculated so that the debt is repaid (amortized) by a specific date.

Interest rates may also be negotiable. As long as you adhere to the terms of the loan you can generally be assured that no payments other than the regular installment ones will be required before the due date of the loan.

If the periodic payments do not completely amortize the debt by the maturity date, the final payment will be larger than the previous periodic payments. This larger, final payment is known as a "balloon" payment. Term loans sometimes allow early repayment without penalty.

Most term loans are only offered to companies with profit histories whose current or projected financial statements demonstrate an ability to repay. The term loan usually requires a written loan agreement that, among other things, might limit your company's other debts, owner salaries, and dividend payments. In addition the agreement may require that a stipulated percentage of company profits must be used to increase repayment installments on the loan, otherwise the loan may be considered in default. Compensating balances are also frequently required.

Term loans also have an advantage in that they develop a lender/borrower relationship over a number of years that can be useful in future financial matters, including advice from the lender concerning preferential future financing arrangements that you could make.

Sometimes personal term loans (in addition to business loans) are available to help finance your initial equity investment in the business. However, this can be risky since the total interest cost on all loans (since little or none of the start up money is your own) can be crippling to the company's working capital.

2. Installment financing

Installment financing could be used to finance the purchase of equipment of various kinds, including automotive equipment, and fixtures (such as counters, shelves, and display cases) where term loans are unavailable.

By using an equipment loan you can retain precious working capital. Lenders will generally finance from 60% to 80% of the equipment's value. The balance is your down payment.

Although some furniture and equipment sales companies may finance this way directly, others will sell to a financing company that, in turn, will do the installment financing.

Many supply companies will act as an intermediary between you and the finance company to coordinate the arrangement. In other cases you may have to shop around to arrange your own installment financing.

Since the assets being financed generally have a life averaging five to ten years, and since the financing agency runs a relatively high risk because of the very low value of second-hand furniture and equipment (and thus its low value as collateral), the length of life of such financing is usually from three to seven years with repayments of principal and interest made monthly.

There is usually a sizable down payment on such arrangements (from 20% to 30%), and the interest rate is generally much higher than with term loans; it could run as much as five or six points over prime.

Installment loans of this type are generally secured by a chattel mortgage (a lien on the assets financed), which can be registered and which permits the seller or lending company to sell the liened assets if the installment payments are in default.

Alternatively, the lender's security could be a conditional sales contract, whereby the seller or lender retains title to the assets until you have satisfied all the terms of the contract.

A cyclical or seasonal business (such as a construction company, or a motel) might have difficulty obtaining an installment loan since a current ratio of 2 to 1 or higher is important in order to obtain such a loan, particularly if the business has fluctuating earnings.

The installment loan agreement also usually binds you to maintaining working capital at an agreed level and to obtain lender approval before making any other capital expenditure for your business over a specified limit. It might also limit the amount that can be paid in salaries and bonuses, and require that assets be kept free of encumbrances. Finally, the agreement might require that a proportion of profits be applied to loan repayments above and beyond the amount stipulated in your note payable securing the loan.

Installment financing does not have to be limited to new equipment. It can also be used to finance used equipment whose original financing has been paid off. In such cases as much as 60% of the equipment's present appraised value may be raised in cash to be repaid in monthly installments over the remaining term of the equipment's useful life.

b. LONG-TERM FINANCING

Where long-term debt is required it will probably be in the form of a mortgage.

A mortgage is a grant, by the borrower to a creditor or lender, of preference or priority in a particular asset. This asset is usually some type of real estate.

When loans are secured by a mortgage the value of the real estate that is the security is not always the only factor considered by the lender. Lenders know, from experience, that there is some risk involved in making mortgage loans on certain types of buildings, particularly on special purpose ones such as a manufacturing plant or a motel that cannot easily be adapted to any other use.

For this reason, other than in the case of a new business, the track record of the borrower over a number of years and the probability of being able to repay the debt as indicated by past financial statements is often given as much weight as the value of the property mortgaged.

If the borrower is in default (for example, for nonpayment of interest and/or principal owing), the creditor holding the mortgage is entitled to force the sale of the specific asset or assets pledged as security.

Proceeds of the sale would go to the holder of the first mortgage before any other creditors would receive anything.

If another creditor had a mortgage on the same asset or assets, he or she would be classified as a second mortgage holder, and would rank below the first mortgage holder but above a third mortgage holder (if one existed) or other creditors of the borrower in default.

The legal procedure by which the first mortgage holder can force the sale is called foreclosure.

In the business world first mortgage lenders are generally organizations that have collected savings from many individual investors or lenders. The organization, acting as an intermediary, combines these savings and lends them in lump sums.

Such organizations are insurance companies, pension companies, real estate investment trusts, commercial and mortgage banks, and even trust companies and credit unions.

1. Feasibility studies and other requirements

Before lending money, these organizations would consider factors such as your past business experience. If you had a proven record of five years or more of successful experience you would more likely be able to obtain funds at a reasonable rate than would a novice.

Lenders are also concerned about the amount of equity invested by you and other owners. This equity usually takes the form of a direct cash investment or purchase of shares if the company is incorporated. Without such equity investment, the mortgage lender is taking a very high-risk position. Generally, such equity needs to be a minimum of 25% to 30% of total company financing.

A prospective lender would also be concerned that proper accounting procedures, particularly for cost control, will be instituted. Lenders frequently require audited financial statements at least yearly but sometimes more frequently. This allows them to read possible danger signs before it is too late.

Some lenders carry out on-site inspections of properties in which they have mortgage investments to ensure that the property is not run down and that it is being maintained adequately. This ensures that their investment is better protected. In some cases the mortgage investor may stipulate a percentage of annual revenue that must be spent on property maintenance.

2. Loan terms

Generally, first mortgages can be obtained for up to 70% or 75% of the appraised value of the land and building offered as security for the loan. If the land is leased, then the mortgage would usually be obtainable only on the appraised value of the building.

Loan terms usually range for a maximum of 20 to 25 years. However, the term could be as short as 10 years.

Repayment of loans is generally made in equal monthly payments of principal and interest. These payments are calculated so that, at the stated interest rate, the regular payments will completely amortize (pay off) the mortgage by the end of its life.

Sometimes the payments are calculated so that, during the early years, interest only is paid (with no reduction in principal).

3. Early prepayment

Most first mortgage loans do not permit any early prepayment for at least the first several years. Thus you are locked in for that period and cannot benefit if interest rates decline.

Where prepayment is allowed, the lender may impose a penalty. The penalty is usually a percentage of the balance still owing, and the percentage may decline as time goes by. You might be prepared to pay such a penalty.

For example, if the initial mortgage carried an 18% interest rate, and current rates had declined to 14%, you might be able to negotiate a new loan with a new lender and use part of the proceeds to pay off the remaining balance of the initial mortgage plus penalty. The penalty imposition may be more than offset by the interest reduction over the term of the new mortgage.

Since circumstances in each case will differ, each decision about long-term mortgage refinancing must be made on its own merits.

4. Call provision

Just as you may be permitted early repayment opportunities to benefit from changed general market interest rates, so too the lender is usually protected. Most mortgage agreements have a call provision in them.

This call provision allows the lender, after a stated number of years, to ask for complete repayment of the mortgage. The lender and borrower then renegotiate a new mortgage at a new interest rate for a further stipulated period of time. A lender would probably call a loan if interest rates had increased since the original mortgage agreement was signed.

There is also an increasing trend toward variable interest rate mortgages where the interest rate, depending on market conditions, can be changed up or down by the lender as frequently as monthly.

5. Other compensation

Some lenders also require additional compensation such as a fee, discount, or bonus. For example, a $10,000 bonus on a $250,000 mortgage would mean you receive only $240,000 but must pay back principal and interest on the $250,000. Such front-end "loads" obviously raise the effective interest rate.

Other lenders may ask for an equity participation. This equity participation increases the lender's return on his investment and, at the same time, dilutes your return on investment. Equity might take the form of a percentage of annual revenue, or an investment in common shares.

6. Joint venture

In some cases the lender might enter into a joint venture agreement with you. Such an agreement might provide you with some equity funds (while giving up part of equity control) as well as mortgage funds.

In other cases the mortgage investor might supply 100% of the total project cost for which he or she receives a substantial equity position. This might significantly reduce your capital outlay and at the same time reduce your risk, control, and potential future income.

7. Equipment and fixtures

Most long-term mortgage lenders will not normally finance any portion of the equipment and fixtures. The prime reason is that mortgage lenders are in the long-term loan business, and furniture and equipment have a relatively short-term life.

However, despite this, they will sometimes attempt to obtain a first mortgage on these chattels (in addition to the long-term mortgage on the assets that they have financed). In this way, if the first mortgage lender has to foreclose, he or she is sure that the equipment and fixtures will not be removed and that the business can continue to operate.

8. Second mortgages

Second mortgages are also used for financing land and building. A second mortgage lender would take a second lien on the property mortgaged. The loan amount is generally limited to 5% to 15% of the appraised value of the property, and loan terms usually range from 5 to 15 years.

Second mortgage interest rates are generally three to four points above first mortgage rates because of the additional risk involved. Repayments are made by you over the life of the loan by way of equal monthly installments of principal and interest.

An excessive second mortgage can be risky to both you and the lender because of potential cash flow problems if the business is not successful.

9. Refinancing

If your property already has a mortgage on it that has been running for some years, you might want to consider refinancing it to raise required funds.

By refinancing, a new mortgage is written based on the present value of the property. You will receive in cash the difference between the old and the new mortgage and make your loan payments on the new mortgage. Since these payments will likely be higher than the previous ones you must be sure that the increased borrowing is used to generate additional long-run profits. It is extremely risky to remortgage your property in order to raise working capital — and lenders are unlikely to take that risk.

9
SOURCES OF FUNDING

Financing is available from a wide selection of commercial sources. It is also available from government sources (to be discussed later).

The wise loan shopper should also realize that commercial lenders (the ones in business primarily for a profit) consider risk the most important factor when establishing interest rates, whereas the main objective of government agencies is to aid small business. Because of this their funds are in limited supply.

You must shop around to locate the type of loan that suits your business's needs and then match that with the appropriate source, keeping the interest rate in mind but realizing that, as a small business, you often have little choice. Some of the major sources of financing are discussed below.

a. BANKS

The most visible and numerous lenders are the commercial banks. They are also the most conservative. It is said that they will do their best to lend you an umbrella, but if it rains demand that you return it immediately.

Banks probably provide about 80% of all business loans. Although they often want plenty of security and proof of cash flow and ability to repay, they are also influenced by a business's profitability, management expertise, and track record.

Banks require a certain amount of owner equity in the business — for example, 25% — before they will consider advancing funds. These funds will be primarily for working capital purposes (financing inventory and accounts receivable), or in the form of short- or medium-term loans for capital purchases.

Banks also offer a line of credit. This line could be up to 65% or 70% of all accounts receivable not over 60 days old, 40% to 45% of inventory value, or 35% to 40% of the appraised value of fixed assets (although the latter is rare).

Their security could be on real or personal property, inventory of any kind, or even the equipment used in the manufacturing or processing of goods.

The amounts that can be borrowed from banks, as well as their interest rates, can be negotiated. Usually the higher the amount to be borrowed, given adequate security, the lower the rate. The rate will usually be about three to four points over prime for the small business operator.

With banks it is sometimes preferable to go to the local main office rather than to a branch. Your own branch office may service the loan, but if the loan is of any size, the main office will have to approve it anyway. In some cases the local main office may itself have to have approval from the regional head office.

Since banks are very conservative lenders they will check your credit standing through trade creditors, other banks you may have done business with, and credit bureaus. They also put great emphasis on your financial statements (balance sheet and income statement), and prefer audited ones.

If you do borrow from a bank after the bank has checked you out, you can be sure that your business is on a fairly solid footing. However, remember that banks do make mistakes!

b. COMMERCIAL FINANCE COMPANIES

A new, or rapidly expanding, small business may find a commercial bank unwilling to lend money because of such factors as lack of track record, a large amount of financing required, or a high debt to equity ratio. An established business may run into the same kind of problems with commercial banks because of the banks' conservatism.

In such cases you may need to seek out commercial finance companies that offer many of the services offered by commercial banks. Commercial finance companies, like banks, are concerned with your ability to repay a loan, but they are more likely to rely on your business's collateral quality than track record or forecast profits and cash flow. They may also be more flexible than commercial banks.

Commercial finance companies offer both accounts receivable and inventory financing, as well as term loans up to five years secured by new equipment. They may also finance used equipment to the extent that equity in fully owned equipment can be used instead of a cash down payment on new equipment purchases.

Commercial finance companies might also offer term loans up to 10 years secured by commercial or industrial real estate, including both first and second mortgage refinancing.

Some more venturesome finance companies have been known to provide partially or totally unsecured long-term loans of from two to ten years based on their assessment of a company's profitability and cash flow rather than on collateral.

Commercial finance companies are also involved in equipment leasing and factoring, as well as sale and lease-back of equipment — financial investments that a commercial bank would seldom, if ever, be involved in.

However, since commercial finance companies run higher risks than banks, and because they frequently borrow some of the money they lend from those banks, their interest rates are usually higher than bank rates.

c. SAVINGS AND LOAN ASSOCIATIONS

Savings and loan associations are primarily in the commercial, industrial and personal real estate financing business.

They will generally make mortgages available for as little as $10,000, advancing up to 75% or 80% of the property value and allowing repayment periods for as long as 25 years. Interest rates vary as the mortgage market varies, and their interest rates are competitive with banks, commercial finance companies, and life insurance companies.

They will deal with both customers and noncustomers but are concerned with the appraised value of the property, its marketability, and location. As is true of commercial banks they dislike very specialized types of manufacturing business and rely heavily on the borrower's personal and business financial statements and proof of ability to pay.

d. FACTORS

A factor is a company that evaluates the credit and collection potential of the accounts receivable of a business and, if considered satisfactory, takes over those accounts and assumes responsibility for collection.

If you factor your accounts, you are paid cash by the factor company while your customers continue to benefit from the normal credit terms that you allow.

Factors do not make loans. They simply purchase your accounts for their perceived value, usually advancing up to 80% of their worth and pay you the remainder (less their factor fee and interest charges) when they collect from your customers.

Generally speaking they deal in short-term accounts receivable of 30 to 90 days and do not handle long-term installment sales. They may at times extend receivable time to six months and extend medium-term loans to regular customers and secure these loans with warehouse receipts or similar collateral.

If a factor assumes your accounts receivable without recourse, this means that it will absorb any bad debt losses and assume the risk, although the factor may hold back from payment to you when a purchaser refuses to pay for faulty merchandise or under similar circumstances.

The factor's fee varies from 1% to 2% of the invoice plus interest on the money advanced to you. This cost is generally higher than either bank or commercial finance company rates for financing your own receivables.

Factors look for a reputable business operator who has reliable customers who pay promptly. In addition they do not like to have receivables concentrated in one or two large accounts. They also like to be sure you honor warranties, service sales, and handle customer complaints satisfactorily.

e. LIFE INSURANCE COMPANIES

Life insurance companies can sometimes be useful as a source of cash when you borrow on your policy. In addition, life insurance companies also offer commercial mortgages (even if you are not a policy holder) as well as unsecured term loans to what they consider safe businesses.

1. Life insurance policies

Before a life insurance policy can be used to raise cash it must generally have been in effect for two years at which point you may borrow up to 95% of its cash value for an indeterminate period. Interest is normally charged yearly but may be deferred indefinitely as long as you continue to regularly pay your insurance premiums.

However, recognize that your loan erodes the dollar value of the insurance policy and your coverage will only be the amount you have not borrowed.

Since policy loans are based on paid-in cash, and thus require little risk from the insurance company, they often provide loans at interest rates less than the banks' prime rate.

2. Mortgages

For long-term mortgage loans, life insurance companies are only generally interested in a minimum period of 15 years or more. Because of this their interest rates have been traditionally lower than other sources. They may also want an option to buy shares in companies to which they lend money. Principal and interest payments are generally payable monthly, as is typical of most mortgages.

Life insurance mortgage loans are frequently handled through independent loan agents such as mortgage bankers. The mortgage loan banker, for a loan service fee, acts as the intermediary between you and the insurance company. Up to 75% of the appraised value of the property can be borrowed this way.

f. CONSUMER FINANCE COMPANIES

When other sources of debt financing are unavailable many small business owners have used consumer finance companies on a personal loan basis.

Consumer or personal finance companies can provide loans as high or higher than $25,000 that can be used to finance a small business. Smaller loans of $5,000 to $10,000 may be secured by personal assets (such as a car).

In the case of loans over $10,000, your home is the security, even if it is already mortgaged, since the loan company will take out a second mortgage on the equity balance beyond the first mortgage. Payment periods vary from a few months up to a few years.

Some consumer finance companies offer unsecured or signature loans in addition to their secured loans. These loans are normally only made to customers with excellent credit ratings.

Consumer finance companies base their loans on the creditworthiness of the individual and the liquidation value of security offered. Applicants are usually required to supply current and past personal credit and other financial data. If your business is the cash source for loan repayment, you will have to provide cash flow statements to demonstrate ability to repay.

Consumer loan companies usually take care of those who are unable to obtain bank or similar credit. Therefore, they are high risk lenders and their interest rates are considerably higher than bank rates for a similar loan.

g. CREDIT UNIONS

Credit unions are becoming a popular source of funds for small businesses. To obtain funds you must be a member and leave on deposit with them in a share account a nominal amount of $25 or $30 that cannot be withdrawn during the term of the loan.

Although short-term loans are preferred, credit unions will make longer loans secured by a real property mortgage. Their rates are competitive with those of commercial banks.

h. VENTURE CAPITAL

There are a number of investment organizations known as venture capital companies who specialize in funding small business. The term small, in this case, does not mean really small. Generally, venture capitalists are only interested in making loans in the $100,000 to $500,000 range for any single venture.

Since these investment companies are more interested in financing ongoing companies, rather than funding brand new ventures, they might well be interested in helping you with the purchase of a successful ongoing business, particularly if you have plans to expand it.

Venture capital is available from these companies in both debt and equity form although it is more common for them to take an equity position (common or preferred shares) since that allows them to participate more easily in the extra profits from the growth of your company.

Under normal circumstances, despite their equity position, venture capitalists are not interested in involvement in the day-to-day operations of your business unless it is having difficulty meeting its obligations. In that case they may well seek a say in management.

However, they might nevertheless seek controls to safeguard their investment. These controls might include the right to veto large capital expenditures, to approve management salaries, to have the final decision on loans over and above normal day-to-day financing, and similar matters. Decisions affecting the general financial situation of your company are very important to the venture capitalist.

Normally they would look for a 20% a year compound rate of growth in your profits and a good likelihood of capital gain on their share holdings in your company by selling their shares in a few years so that they can invest the proceeds in new investments. Sometimes this divestment of their shares takes place progressively as your company matures.

Extracting funds from venture capitalists is not easy. They receive many more applications from people than they can ever fund. You will have to prepare a well documented financial plan when approaching a venture capital company.

Some venture capital companies are affiliated with banks and similar financial institutions, insurance companies, and some large corporations looking for diversification. Other venture capitalists are groups of wealthy individuals or families and private groups of investors who have pooled their resources to seek out healthy investments.

Selling common stock to venture capital companies can be an expensive form of financing. If your business prospers through your hard work it is sometimes frustrating to see much of the reward going to others through a financial commitment made earlier. Before approaching a venture capital company you should perhaps explore all other avenues of financing that do not mean giving up an equity share.

1. Requirements

Management is the key to the success of any small business, regardless of the product or service it sells. Therefore, the quality of your management is a major factor in attracting favorable attention from venture capitalists.

Venture capital investors are also looking for a better product or service — one that has a competitive advantage. They would be keenly interested in a new idea or product, supported by market and competition analysis showing that it has a good chance of success.

Venture capital companies are looking for investments in businesses in industries that are growing rapidly.

Finally, cash flow is critical. Many small business operators have their priorities back to front ranking their objectives as growth first, profits second, and cash flow third. If the business grows faster than the cash flow it will soon run out of cash and be unable to pay its debts. The venture capital investor is looking for the business owner who can balance growth in sales with profits and cash flow and understands the importance of cash flow to allow the company to expand using internally generated financing.

2. Suppliers

One source of venture capital apart from friends and relatives on the one hand, and the major venture investment companies on the other, are the major suppliers of the product you are dealing with. This is particularly true if you are in the wholesale or retail business.

By providing financing for you your supplier may be able to obtain a larger market share and thus provide your venture capital for either start-up or expansion costs. This type of venture financing can sometimes be obtained at little or no cost since the supplier's return will come through increased sales to you.

Your bank manager or loan officer should be able to direct you to venture capital companies in your area.

i. SMALL BUSINESS ADMINISTRATION (U.S.)

If all else fails, you might want to consider the U.S. Small Business Administration (SBA). The SBA was created in 1953 by the federal government to succeed several predecessor agencies responsible for assisting entrepreneurs. Since that date SBA has endured and expanded to embrace many activities. Its functions include, among others, finance and investment.

The SBA is organized into 10 regions and each region is subdivided, providing district or branch offices in many areas. As the lender of final resort the SBA tries not to compete with or replace the private banking system but to supplement it.

SBA guidelines defining who qualifies for small business assistance vary, depending on the general classification of the enterprise. At the present time, the eligibility of businesses is measured by sales volume or revenue. For example, the upper limit is $3 million per year for retail/service businesses.

Loans made by SBA generally mature in 10 years or less for fixtures and equipment, and are repaid in equal monthly installments of principal and interest, although this time period may be extended to 20 years where the purchase of land and/or a building are concerned. Working capital loans can be made for periods up to six years. Regardless of the loan term, the loan may be repaid at any time prior to maturity without penalty.

There are three types of loans available from the SBA: guaranteed loans, immediate participation loans, and direct loans.

1. Guaranteed loans

Since the philosophy of the SBA is that the private banking industry is the basic mechanism for the distribution of debt financing to small business, loans are made to a business by a bank or similar lending institution, but at a reduced risk because the SBA guarantees to pay part of any loss the lending bank might suffer.

Under the guaranteed loan arrangement up to 90% of a loan may be guaranteed, or $500,000 — whichever is less.

The interest rate charged by a bank for a guaranteed loan may not exceed the prime rate by more than 2¼% for loans of less than seven years maturity, and the prime rate plus 2¾% for loans of over seven years.

The actual interest rate is negotiable, but the majority of loans tend to be near the high end of the range. In rare cases it may be possible to borrow at or even below the prime rate. This could occur in a chain franchise operation because of the financial strength of the franchisor.

2. Immediate participation loans

In cases where a guaranteed loan cannot be arranged, an immediate participation loan may be available. With this type of loan, the SBA and the bank each provide a portion of the loan. For example, the bank may lend the major share of the funds required and be permitted to charge interest up to 2¾% over prime.

This interest rate is negotiable and could even be a fluctuating rate as market conditions change. The balance of the loan is from the SBA and its interest cost is based on the government's cost of funds but by statute cannot exceed a rate that is 1% less than the maximum rate banks are allowed to charge on guaranteed SBA loans.

3. Direct loans

Direct loans are generally arranged at interest rates considerably less than those on SBA sponsored bank loans. Direct loans may not exceed $150,000 without special approval, and in no case can they exceed the maximum limit of $350,000 established by statute.

Since direct loans are derived from a limited pool of funds, the availability of those loans is quite restricted. In the majority of cases, application for a direct loan is only made after the prospective borrower has demonstrated that credit is not otherwise available.

Since the SBA's regulations do change from time to time you should verify current conditions by contacting your nearest branch of the SBA (listed in your telephone directory under U.S. Government) or write to:

Small Business Administration
Washington, DC 20416

j. FEDERAL BUSINESS DEVELOPMENT BANK (CANADA)

In Canada you should also be aware of the Federal Business Development Bank, or FBDB. This lender is sometimes referred to as the lender of last resort. It was established by the government especially to help those companies that could not obtain financing elsewhere.

If your funding application has been turned down by other financial institutions, you may apply to the FBDB.

To obtain FBDB financing the amount of your investment in the business must generally be sufficient to ensure that you are committed to it and that the business may reasonably be expected to be successful.

FBDB financing is available by means of loans, loan guarantees, equity financing, leasing, or by any combination of these methods, in whatever way best suits the particular needs of your business. If loans are involved, they are usually at interest rates in line with those of other banks. If equity is involved, the FBDB generally takes a minority interest and is prepared to have you buy back its equity on suitable terms when the business is able to do this.

Most of the FBDB's customers use funds to acquire land, buildings, or equipment, although it is possible to use those funds to provide a healthy working capital for the business.

Financing from the FBDB can range from a few thousand to $100,000. Not many loans are made in excess of that amount. The amount that can be borrowed for a specific purpose depends on your ability to satisfy the bank's general requirements.

Also, once you have arranged financing from the FBDB there is nothing to prevent you from returning and requesting further funding at a later date. If you wish to pursue this, contact your local branch of the FBDB, or write to:

Federal Business Development Bank
901 Victoria Square
Montreal, Quebec
H2Z 1R1

10
FINANCIAL PLAN

The size of a business has a bearing on the amount of financing it needs. Generally, the smaller the business the less its financial requirements. As a business grows, so will its financial needs and the variety of possible reasons for needing funding.

a. REASONS FOR FINANCING

There are a number of different reasons why companies need money, such as to start up a new business, to provide working capital, to handle a seasonal peak, to purchase new equipment and facilities, to finance remodeling, to finance growth of your company, and to enlarge or add to your premises.

1. Starting a new business

To start a new business will require a different amount of financing depending on the type of business, whether premises can be rented or must be built or purchased, the amount of start-up inventory that must be purchased, and the amount of working capital required until cash can be generated from sales.

A new business has to be fairly precise in its projections of investment required, as well as forecasts of revenue and expenses over the initial months, and possibly even years, to indicate if the business will be profitable.

A cash flow plan must be part of the overall projections since that will show, among other things, whether or not cash will be generated to repay any loans made to start up the business.

The larger the business, and the more that has to be borrowed, the more detailed the financial plan will have to be, since lenders are not going to be sympathetic to a request for funding supported by figures scratched out on the back of an envelope.

Businesses with the highest start-up costs are generally those requiring a manufacturing process, high technology, and sophisticated production systems. These require specific types or sizes of buildings and expensive equipment and machinery.

A retail business, on the other hand, may require much less initial investment, particularly if it is in leased premises. However, if you own the land, construct a building, and invest heavily in equipment, fixtures, and inventory, the start-up costs can also be quite high.

A service business (barber shop, real estate company, employment agency, tradesperson) may require little or no initial investment and, in some cases, can be operated out of a home.

If the business can be started with little or no borrowed money then, when it is proved successful, financing from outside sources will be easier and the advantages of leverage can be used.

2. Working capital requirements

Both new businesses and ongoing businesses need money for working capital. This working capital is for purchasing inventory, carrying receivables, and similar ongoing situations. Working capital has been discussed in some detail in earlier chapters, as have methods for financing current assets such as accounts receivable and inventory.

3. Seasonal peak

Funding required for a seasonal or cyclical business usually involves working capital accounts. In other words, a business borrows short-term funds prior to the production-sales peak period and repays later when the increased inventory has been converted into receivables and then into cash. These cyclical or seasonal requirements for peak periods can best be forecast using cash budgeting (see chapter 4).

One of the risks with seasonal financing is that inventory will not sell as well as predicted. This may leave a business with an unsold inventory and an inability to repay loans.

4. New equipment and/or facilities

When a business needs to replace old equipment or add to its present equipment it often has to borrow money, or borrow at least part of it. This type of cash requirement is of an intermediate-term type, and you should not use working capital funds for that.

5. Remodeling

Remodeling can be a major occasion for financial borrowing. Remodeling should only occur if it will also improve sales. After remodeling, costs will probably also increase but that increase should be less than the increase in sales.

6. Sales growth

If your business is expanding rapidly through sales growth, you may need funds to carry a larger inventory, increase production, add employees to your payroll, and even add equipment.

Frequently the funding for this type of expansion cannot be financed from internal operations and money of various types may be required. This money could come from short-term or intermediate-term sources.

Since under rapid growth a seasonal business may face as many problems as a new business starting up it is important that rapid growth be anticipated and that a detailed financing plan be prepared well in advance so that appropriate funding can be arranged.

7. Enlarging or adding to premises

If you are adding to or enlarging your premises, it is likely that you will have to provide much of the money for this from outside lenders. This type of funding is long-term and projections of increased profits and cash flow must show that you can afford to pay back both interest and principal on this type of borrowing.

b. FINANCIAL PLANNING

Financial planning is not something that happens only intermittently. Although major investments, such as starting a new business or expanding your premises, do not occur regularly, other parts of financing, such as funding working capital, expanding sales, and anticipating seasonal variations, are an ongoing process.

For example, every well-managed business prepares a budget or financial plan at least once a year. This budget aids you in operating your business in the coming year by forcing you to appraise your business to ensure that all of its aspects are evaluated for the next 12 months.

Your budget may even show you that you must also prepare a financial plan to obtain financing for an anticipated change in your business. The first question you must ask when seeking financing is the specific reason you need it. The reason or reasons will probably be found in the categories discussed earlier.

The next step is to determine how much money is needed since that is the first question that any potential lender is going to ask you.

The third step is to decide how any borrowed money is going to be repaid. Regardless of whether you approach friends, a local banker, or a major investment company, they will want some statement, and preferably documentation, about how the money can be paid back out of profits and cash flow, and over what period of time.

In particular, if money is in short supply and interest rates high, and the reason for seeking financing can be deferred, then that is a decision you might want to make. You must be sure that you can afford the cost of any borrowed money. In other words, the income it generates must exceed expenses, and cash flow must be adequate to pay back any loan with interest. You must be confident about that before making the final commitment to borrow money.

1. What's involved in financing?

Knowing what's involved in securing financing can give you a distinct advantage. The most important fact to remember is that you are in competition with other people and other businesses for the same money.

It is often said that there is a shortage of funds for financing small businesses. However, what is more the case is that many small business planners, owners, or operators are unfamiliar with the range of sources of funds and financial services available to them.

Another common complaint is that banks and other financial institutions turn down funding requests by insisting on 100% guarantees of the success of the business venture when the real reason is that they were just not provided with sufficient documented information to make a positive decision.

Therefore, being prepared, understanding the procedures involved, and having familiarity with the different types of financing available are the first steps in demonstrating good management of a financial proposal.

2. Competition among lenders

You should also understand that banks and other financial institutions are no different than you: they are in competition with each other in the same way you are with your competitors.

Banks make money by lending money out at a profit. If they don't lend money, they don't make that profit. However, for business to be profitable to the bank, the bank has to assess the risk in lending its money.

In borrowing money the words risk and interest are closely connected. Risk is the degree of danger the lender has in losing funds loaned to you. Interest is what you pay a lender for the use of borrowed funds. Normally, the higher the risk, the higher the interest rate.

Decisions made by bankers are based on their judgment of the viability of your proposal. This judgment follows no secret formulas (since banks do make errors in lending money that they cannot collect). However, bankers do use certain basic information to determine risk and make decisions. This basic information is usually derived from data provided in your loan application.

c. PREPARING THE PAPERWORK

The style and content of a loan application are of major importance when asking for a loan. To make the best impression on those approached for funding it is critical to have all the facts properly documented. Regardless of the type of loan, the information required by the lender will be basically the same.

The lender will want to know who you are, what your plans are, and what these plans will do for the business. The preparation of this information in answer to the lender's questions, and the analysis that backs it up, is quite simple. A systematized approach to preparing this information for a lender you have not previously dealt with should include the following items.

1. Resume of the owner

The lender will want to know something about you (and any other owners) such as your education and experience (or lack of it) and how this will be valuable to the business.

The lender will want to be assured of your managerial skills. A past track record demonstrating ability in matters such as production, marketing, financing, and similar areas and how these can be related to the business you are in are some determining factors in assessing your management ability.

In essence the lender needs this information to size up your character (as well as that of any other partners or shareholders in the business), honesty, reliability, trustworthiness, responsibility, willingness to work, and wise use of any borrowed funds.

The lender can then compare, from his or her own experience in loaning money to other businesses, the relative strengths of your case.

2. Personal financial information

If you do not have a previous business track record, the lender will probably need personal financial information about you and the other owners. This information will show the lender what other financial support you can fall back on if the business runs into difficulty and requires further owner investment. A personal financial information form is illustrated in Sample #10.

3. References

You will probably need to provide references, both personal and business. If you have dealt with other banks previously references from them can be helpful, including details of any previous or present loans outstanding with those banks. The names of your accountant and lawyer are also useful for references.

4. Products and/or services

The lender will want some details about the products and services of your company. This will include information concerning sales trends of the products, their prices, their quality in comparison with competitors, and any proposed change in the product mix and the effect of that on profits.

The lender is concerned with such matters as the acceptability of your business's products, their diversity, their competitiveness, and the possible problems of borrowed money going into risky new products.

With reference to future prospects the bank might want to consider the impact of environmental and/or technological change on your business. Such factors as the availability of labor (if it is a labor intensive business), consistency of supply of required raw materials, and the adequacy of the present building and equipment to meet your projected future sales would be of concern to the lender.

An assessment of your market, and potential market share could be included at this point. Finally, don't be reticent about including the names of your nearest competitors.

5. Financial statements

Financial statement projections will be required for the next 12 months with detailed calculations showing, in particular, how total annual revenue is calculated and what

SAMPLE #10
PERSONAL FINANCIAL INFORMATION FORM

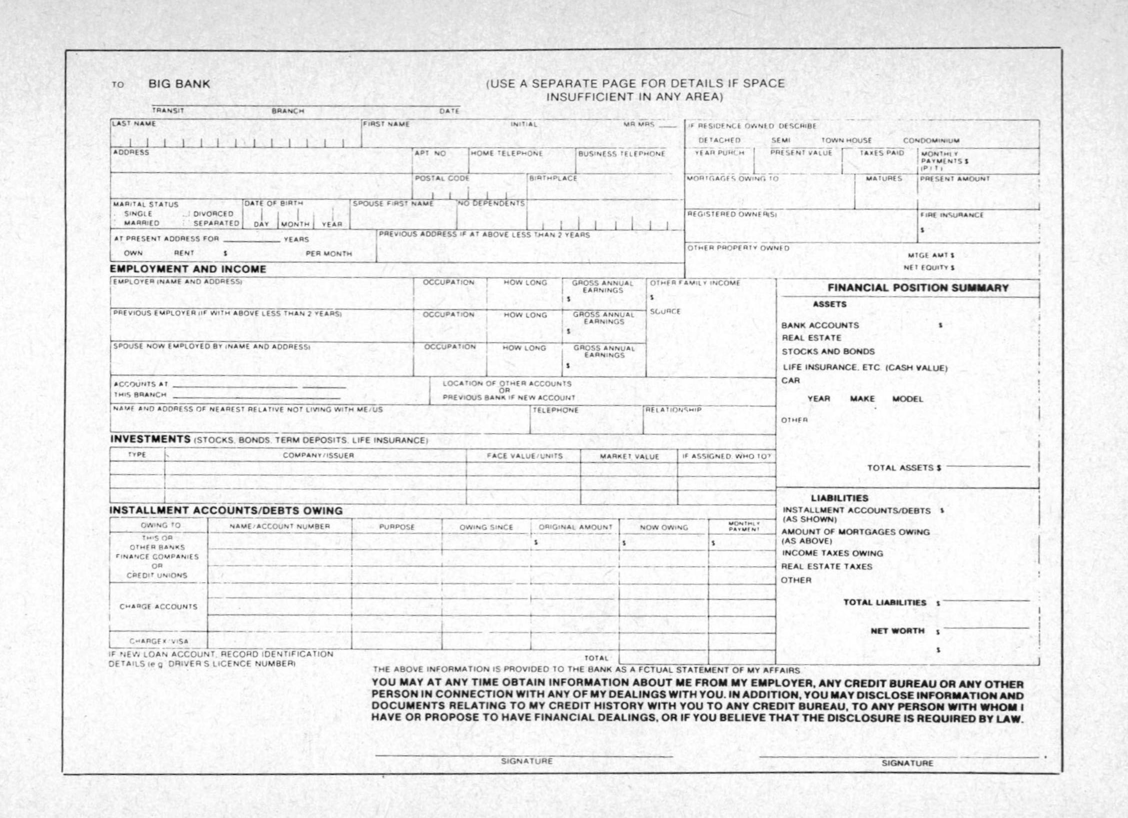

TO BIG BANK

(USE A SEPARATE PAGE FOR DETAILS IF SPACE INSUFFICIENT IN ANY AREA)

TRANSIT BRANCH DATE

LAST NAME | FIRST NAME | INITIAL | MR MRS

ADDRESS | APT NO | HOME TELEPHONE | BUSINESS TELEPHONE

POSTAL CODE | BIRTHPLACE

MARITAL STATUS: SINGLE, MARRIED, DIVORCED, SEPARATED | DATE OF BIRTH: DAY, MONTH, YEAR | SPOUSE FIRST NAME | NO DEPENDENTS

AT PRESENT ADDRESS FOR ______ YEARS
OWN RENT $ PER MONTH

PREVIOUS ADDRESS IF AT ABOVE LESS THAN 2 YEARS

IF RESIDENCE OWNED DESCRIBE
DETACHED SEMI TOWN HOUSE CONDOMINIUM

YEAR PURCH | PRESENT VALUE | TAXES PAID | MONTHLY PAYMENTS $ (P.I.T.)

MORTGAGES OWING TO | MATURES | PRESENT AMOUNT

REGISTERED OWNER(S) | FIRE INSURANCE $

OTHER PROPERTY OWNED
MTGE AMT $
NET EQUITY $

EMPLOYMENT AND INCOME

EMPLOYER (NAME AND ADDRESS)	OCCUPATION	HOW LONG	GROSS ANNUAL EARNINGS $
PREVIOUS EMPLOYER (IF WITH ABOVE LESS THAN 2 YEARS)	OCCUPATION	HOW LONG	GROSS ANNUAL EARNINGS $
SPOUSE NOW EMPLOYED BY (NAME AND ADDRESS)	OCCUPATION	HOW LONG	GROSS ANNUAL EARNINGS $

OTHER FAMILY INCOME $
SOURCE

ACCOUNTS AT THIS BRANCH ______

LOCATION OF OTHER ACCOUNTS OR PREVIOUS BANK IF NEW ACCOUNT

NAME AND ADDRESS OF NEAREST RELATIVE NOT LIVING WITH ME/US | TELEPHONE | RELATIONSHIP

INVESTMENTS (STOCKS, BONDS, TERM DEPOSITS, LIFE INSURANCE)

TYPE	COMPANY/ISSUER	FACE VALUE/UNITS	MARKET VALUE	IF ASSIGNED, WHO TO?

INSTALLMENT ACCOUNTS/DEBTS OWING

OWING TO	NAME/ACCOUNT NUMBER	PURPOSE	OWING SINCE	ORIGINAL AMOUNT	NOW OWING	MONTHLY PAYMENT
THIS OR OTHER BANKS FINANCE COMPANIES OR CREDIT UNIONS				$	$	$
CHARGE ACCOUNTS						
CHARGEX/VISA						
				TOTAL		

IF NEW LOAN ACCOUNT, RECORD IDENTIFICATION DETAILS (e.g. DRIVER'S LICENCE NUMBER)

FINANCIAL POSITION SUMMARY

ASSETS
BANK ACCOUNTS $
REAL ESTATE
STOCKS AND BONDS
LIFE INSURANCE, ETC. (CASH VALUE)
CAR
YEAR MAKE MODEL
OTHER
TOTAL ASSETS $

LIABILITIES
INSTALLMENT ACCOUNTS/DEBTS (AS SHOWN) $
AMOUNT OF MORTGAGES OWING (AS ABOVE)
INCOME TAXES OWING
REAL ESTATE TAXES
OTHER
TOTAL LIABILITIES $
NET WORTH $
$

THE ABOVE INFORMATION IS PROVIDED TO THE BANK AS A FCTUAL STATEMENT OF MY AFFAIRS.

YOU MAY AT ANY TIME OBTAIN INFORMATION ABOUT ME FROM MY EMPLOYER, ANY CREDIT BUREAU OR ANY OTHER PERSON IN CONNECTION WITH ANY OF MY DEALINGS WITH YOU. IN ADDITION, YOU MAY DISCLOSE INFORMATION AND DOCUMENTS RELATING TO MY CREDIT HISTORY WITH YOU TO ANY CREDIT BUREAU, TO ANY PERSON WITH WHOM I HAVE OR PROPOSE TO HAVE FINANCIAL DEALINGS, OR IF YOU BELIEVE THAT THE DISCLOSURE IS REQUIRED BY LAW.

SIGNATURE SIGNATURE

the operating costs are projected to be. Forecast cash flow projections, month by month for the next year, will also be required.

You will need to provide past financial statements going back at least three years if you have been in business that long. These financial statements would include income statements, balance sheets, and possibly cash flow statements.

In other words, the lender is interested in how your business is doing, its direction and possible growth and, most important, its ability to repay any loans from cash flow.

In particular the lender will be looking for potential problems indicated by your financial statements. These problems could be matters such as overdue receivables, overvalued inventory, too high inventory in relation to sales, large loans to owners, too high a dividend payout or owner cash withdrawals, a serious possible decline in sales in poor economic times, or too much investment in fixed assets in relation to sales.

The amount of your investment or equity in the business is important. Banks and other lending institutions do not finance 100% of the financial needs of a business. You have to put some of your own money in, as much as 25% of the total cash required.

You might like to show how the required money is going to be used, and the various sources of funding. A very simple plan would look like this:

USE OF FUNDS	
Building addition	$100,000
New equipment	23,000
Contingencies	7,000
Total	$130,000

SOURCE OF FUNDS	
Bank loan	$105,000
Shareholder loan	25,000
Total	$130,000

6. Security offered

The prospective lender will want details of the security offered for any loan. This includes a description of the assets (land, building, equipment and fixtures, accounts receivable, inventory, and even firm sales contracts). If you can offer personal security (house, stocks, bonds, life insurance, and similar items), this too should be listed.

In particular, if you own the land and/or building and there has been a recent appraisal this will be useful since it will indicate what the property is worth.

If the land and/or building are not owned, a lease agreement that you have might form the security offered. In this case a copy of the lease agreement should be provided the lender along with a statement from the landlord showing that all rent payments already made (if any) have been made promptly.

If any of your assets are currently secured against other mortgages or loans, you must provide details such as the specific assets involved, the amount originally borrowed against them, and the amount still outstanding.

The amount of security required by lenders will differ in each case. If a business is stable, mature, and has built up a solid creditworthiness with a lender, the demand for security is lessened. Real estate is generally valued at 75% of its market price, equipment at 50% to 80% depending on its age, and inventory as low as 50%.

For a successful ongoing business a major item of security could be the future earnings potential of the business.

7. Insurance policies

The lender will want to know if the business is adequately insured against losses and liabilities and, in each case, who the beneficiaries are. Therefore, copies of any insurance policies should be made available to the lender.

8. Credit rating

It is important that both you and your business have a good credit rating since lenders (and even suppliers in the case of a new business) will frequently refer to that to help make a decision.

You should contact your local office of a reputable credit reporting agency if you have not already established a credit rating.

Credit reporting agencies will require much of the information outlined above so that they can prepare a brief synopsis of your business and your personal background.

This information should be freely given to ensure that they do have accurate information. Any information they have about you from other sources (suppliers and lenders with whom you have done business, and from personal or business references) is available to you for your inspection.

If it is correctly documented and up-to-date, a credit report can be helpful in influencing a lender who refers to that credit agency for the current report on your credit background.

9. Formal loan plan layout

The following is an outline of a formal loan plan that you can use if required. Many financial lenders, particularly if they are familiar with your business from previous occasions, do not need this type of formal outline but are quite satisfied with the answers to the questions discussed above. But there may be occasions when it is advantageous to follow or adapt the outline format shown in Sample #11.

10. Other considerations

The importance of careful preparation of all the paperwork outlined above cannot be overstressed. The manner in which this information is professionally prepared and presented to a potential lender will go a long way toward ensuring that the required funds will be obtained.

In calculating projected sales and expenses, accuracy is critical. If careless errors are made in overestimating revenue or underestimating expenses (thus producing a padded profit amount), your credibility will be damaged. The chances of obtaining borrowed funds will be considerably decreased. For this reason professional help from a financial consultant or an accountant may be necessary.

Even though a suggested list of paperwork items has been outlined above it might be a good idea to contact

SAMPLE #11
LOAN PLAN OUTLINE

A. Summary

1. Nature of your business
2. Reason for loan and amount required
3. Proposed terms of repayment
4. Amount of additional equity investment and resulting debt/equity ratio
5. Security or collateral for loan

B. Personal Information

1. Your education and business background
2. Credit references
3. Personal income tax statements for past three years
4. Personal financial statements

C. Business Information

1. Brief business history
2. Current balance sheet
3. Income statements for past several years

D. Financial Projections

1. Sales and expense projections for next 12 months, by month
2. Cash flow projections for next 12 months, by month
3. Proposed balance sheet one year hence

(Any necessary explanations should be included with these projections.)

potential lenders, in each specific case, to determine what they would like to be presented with.

This will ensure that time is not needlessly spent putting together a report that is far more than a lender is interested in or, alternatively, a report that fails to include some specific item that the lender does want.

When seeking financing it is a good idea to make appointments in a businesslike way with each potential lender. That is more likely to portray the image of a professional business operator than by just simply walking in the door and asking for money.

d. LENDING DECISIONS

When you are applying for funds there are two possibilities: the funding will be approved or denied.

1. Funding approved

If a request for financing is approved, find out everything you need to know about the conditions, terms, payment methods, interest rates, security requirements, and if there are any front end charges or fees to be paid. No commitment to accept the financing should be made until all this information is provided and understood and its implications considered.

If you are told that financing will be approved if certain other conditions are met, determine if these conditions are severe enough to restrict the operating standards you desire. Will the conditions commit you to more than was intended, or are they normal financing requirements that were simply overlooked?

Once a final commitment is made, it is a good idea to provide the lender with future copies of financial statements. Frequently this will be one of the requirements for obtaining funding. Even if it is not, it will provide the lender with progress reports about the business and will be helpful to the lender in processing future applications for further financing.

2. Funding denied

If a request for financing is not approved, find out why. Use the lender's experience to advantage. He or she will have a reason for not providing the financing. Lenders handle many requests for financing and have experience in the financial aspects (even if they do not have direct management experience) of many businesses.

For example, the lender might be able to see that your business will run into a shortage of working capital with the financial plan proposed. A shortage of working capital is one of the common reasons for failure of many small businesses. If a business is in trouble because of this, it is often difficult to obtain additional working capital assistance.

It is far preferable to ask for additional funds to strengthen working capital at the outset, and a potential lender may well be able to point this out as a possible problem with your proposed financing plan.

If there is something else wrong with the financing proposal, see if it can be corrected and then reapply. If not, use this knowledge when approaching other potential lenders, or on future occasions when seeking funds.

11

LONG-TERM ASSET MANAGEMENT

The money you invest in your small business may be needed to buy fixed or long-term assets. This type of asset is needed to operate the business and is not sold as are products. Included in long-term assets are land, building, equipment and fixtures, and vehicles.

A part of the useful life of each kind of long-term asset (except land) is used up over time as you sell your products and/or services. In other words, most fixed assets generally wear out or deteriorate over time.

The initial value of long-term assets recorded on the balance sheet is the cost or price originally paid. Each income statement period (month, quarter, or year), a part of this cost is deducted from the original cost on the balance sheet and is shown as an expense on the income statement. This expense is normally called depreciation.

Since land does not wear out depreciation is not shown for land nor is it allowed for income tax purposes. For depreciation on the other fixed assets the income tax department has rules that you must follow concerning how, and at what maximum rate, you may depreciate various types of assets for tax filing purposes.

Because these rules can be quite complex, and change from time to time, they are not discussed in this book. Indeed, it is probably a good idea to let your accountant advise you on the current regulations in tax matters such as depreciation.

If you are starting a new business or even expanding an existing one, it may not be a good idea to raise financing for purchase of major assets such as land and building. It may be preferable to lease them. Similarly, equipment and vehicles can be leased to conserve cash. Cash availability is an important ingredient to the financial success of a business in its early months and, in some cases, years. Assets that are leased initially can always be purchased later on. The subject of leasing will be discussed in the next chapter.

a. INVESTING IN LONG-TERM ASSETS

Investment in long-term assets is sometimes referred to as capital budgeting, but we are not so much concerned in this chapter with the budgeting process as we are with the decision about whether or not to make a specific investment, or with the decision about which of two or more investments would be preferable.

1. Differences from day-to-day decisions

Long-term investment decision-making differs from day-to-day decision-making and ongoing budgeting.

For example, long-term investment decisions concern assets that have a relatively long life. Day-to-day decisions concern assets that turn over frequently. A wrong decision about a piece of equipment can involve a time span stretching over many years. A wrong decision about operating supplies has only a short run effect.

Also, day-to-day operating decisions do not usually involve large amounts of money for any individual item, whereas the purchase of a long-term asset requires the outlay of a large sum of money that can have a major effect if a wrong decision is made.

2. Four methods

Four methods of investment decision-making will be discussed:

(a) Average rate of return (ARR)

(b) Payback period (PP)

(c) Net present value (NPV)

(d) Internal rate of return (IRR)

To set the scene for the ARR and the PP methods, let us consider Rita's Retail business that is using a hand system for recording sales.

Rita is investigating the value of installing an electronic register that will eliminate part of the present wage cost and save an estimated $4,000 a year. The register will cost $5,000 and is expected to have a 5-year life with no trade-in value. Depreciation is therefore $1,000 a year ($5,000 divided by 5). Saving and expense figures are:

Saving — employee wages	$4,000
Expenses:	
Maintenance	$ 350
Stationery	650
Depreciation	1,000
Total	$2,000
Saving before tax	$2,000
Income tax	1,000
Net annual saving	$1,000

b. AVERAGE RATE OF RETURN (ARR)

The ARR method compares the average annual net profit (after income tax) resulting from the investment with the average investment. The formula for the ARR is:

$$\frac{\text{Net annual saving}}{\text{Average investment}}$$

Note that the average investment is simply initial investment divided by two. Using the information from above, Rita calculated the ARR to be:

$$\frac{\$1,000}{\$(5,000 \div 2)} \times 100 = \frac{\$1,000}{\$2,500} \times 100 = 40.0\%$$

The advantage of the ARR method is its simplicity. It is frequently used to compare the anticipated return from a proposal with a minimum desired return. If the proposal's return is less than desired it is rejected. If greater than desired, a more in-depth analysis, using other investment techniques, might then be used.

The major disadvantage of the ARR is that it is based on net profit rather than on cash flow.

c. PAYBACK PERIOD (PP)

The PP method overcomes the cash flow shortcoming of the ARR. The PP method measures the initial investment with the annual cash inflows. The equation is

$$\frac{\text{Initial investment}}{\text{Net annual cash saving}}$$

Since the information above only gives Rita net annual saving, and not net annual cash saving, Rita must first convert the net annual saving figure to a cash basis. This is done by adding back the depreciation (an expense that does not require an outlay of cash). Rita's cash saving figure is:

Net annual saving	$1,000
Add depreciation	1,000
Net annual cash saving	$2,000

and Rita's payback period is then:

$$\frac{\$5,000}{\$2,000} = 2.5 \text{ years}$$

The PP method, although simple, does not really measure the merits of investments, but only the speed with which the investment cost might be recovered. It has a use in evaluating a number of proposals so that only those that fall within a predetermined payback period will be considered for further evaluation using other investment techniques.

However, both the PP and the ARR methods still suffer from a common fault: they both ignore the time value of cash flows, or the concept that money now is worth more than the same amount of money at some time in the future. This concept will be discussed in the next section, after which we will explore the use of the net present value and internal rate of return methods.

d. DISCOUNTED CASH FLOW

The concept of discounted cash flow can probably best be understood by looking first at an example of compound interest. Sample #12 shows, year by year, what happens to $100 invested at a 10% compound interest rate. At the end of four years, the investment is worth $146.41.

Discounting is simply the reverse of compounding interest. In other words, at a 10% interest rate, what is $146.41 four years from now worth today? The solution can be worked out manually or with a hand calculator, but can much more easily be solved by using a table of discounted cash flow factors.

1. Using discount tables

Sample #13 illustrates a discount table. If you go to the number, called a factor, that is opposite year 4 and under the 10% column, you will see that is is 0.6830. This factor tells us that $1.00 received at the end of year 4 is worth only $1.00 x 0.683 = $0.683 right now.

Indeed, this factor tells us, expressed in a different way, that any amount of money at the end of four years from now at a 10% interest (discount) rate is worth only 68.3% of that amount right now. You can prove this by taking the $146.41 amount at the end of year 4 from Sample #12 and discounting it back to the present:

$146.41 x 0.683 = $99.99803 or $100.00

You know that $100 is the right answer because it is the amount in the illustration of compounding interest in Sample #12.

For a series of annual cash flows, you simply apply the related annual discount factor for that year to the cash inflow for that year. For example, a cash inflow of $1,000 a year for each of three years using a 10% factor will give the following total discounted cash flow:

Year	Factor	Amount	Total
1	0.9091	$1,000	$ 909.10
2	0.8264	$1,000	826.40
3	0.7513	$1,000	751.30
			$2,486.80

SAMPLE #12
EFFECT OF COMPOUNDING INTEREST

	Jan. 1 Year 1	Dec. 31 Year 1	Dec. 31 Year 2	Dec. 31 Year 3	Dec. 31 Year 4
Balance forward	$100.00	$100.00	$110.00	$121.00	$133.10
Interest 10%		10.00	11.00	12.10	13.31
Investment value end of year		$110.00	$121.00	$133.10	$146.41

SAMPLE #13
TABLE OF DISCOUNTED CASH FLOW FACTORS

Year	5%	6%	7%	8%	9%	10%	11%	12%	13%	14%	15%	16%	17%	18%	19%	20%	25%	30%
1	0.9524	0.9434	0.9346	0.9259	0.9174	0.9091	0.9009	0.8929	0.8850	0.8772	0.8696	0.8621	0.8547	0.8475	0.8403	0.8333	0.8000	0.7692
2	0.9070	0.8900	0.8734	0.8573	0.8417	0.8264	0.8116	0.7972	0.7831	0.7695	0.7561	0.7432	0.7305	0.7182	0.7062	0.6944	0.6400	0.5917
3	0.8638	0.8396	0.8163	0.7938	0.7722	0.7513	0.7312	0.7118	0.6931	0.6750	0.6575	0.6407	0.6244	0.6086	0.5934	0.5787	0.5120	0.4552
4	0.8227	0.7921	0.7629	0.7350	0.7084	0.6830	0.6587	0.6355	0.6133	0.5921	0.5718	0.5523	0.5337	0.5158	0.4987	0.4823	0.4096	0.3501
5	0.7835	0.7473	0.7130	0.6806	0.6499	0.6209	0.5935	0.5674	0.5428	0.5194	0.4972	0.4761	0.4561	0.4371	0.4191	0.4019	0.3277	0.2693
6	0.7462	0.7050	0.6663	0.6302	0.5963	0.5645	0.5346	0.5066	0.4803	0.4556	0.4323	0.4104	0.3898	0.3704	0.3521	0.3349	0.2621	0.2072
7	0.7107	0.6651	0.6228	0.5835	0.5470	0.5132	0.4817	0.4524	0.4251	0.3996	0.3759	0.3538	0.3332	0.3139	0.2959	0.2791	0.2097	0.1594
8	0.6768	0.6274	0.5820	0.5403	0.5019	0.4665	0.4339	0.4039	0.3762	0.3506	0.3269	0.3050	0.2848	0.2660	0.2487	0.2326	0.1678	0.1226
9	0.6446	0.5919	0.5439	0.5003	0.4604	0.4241	0.3909	0.3606	0.3329	0.3075	0.2843	0.2630	0.2434	0.2255	0.2090	0.1938	0.1342	0.0943
10	0.6139	0.5584	0.5084	0.4632	0.4224	0.3855	0.3522	0.3220	0.2946	0.2697	0.2472	0.2267	0.2080	0.1911	0.1756	0.1615	0.1074	0.0725
11	0.5847	0.5268	0.4751	0.4289	0.3875	0.3505	0.3173	0.2875	0.2607	0.2366	0.2149	0.1954	0.1778	0.1619	0.1476	0.1346	0.0859	0.0558
12	0.5568	0.4970	0.4440	0.3971	0.3555	0.3186	0.2858	0.2567	0.2307	0.2076	0.1869	0.1685	0.1520	0.1372	0.1240	0.1122	0.0687	0.0429
13	0.5303	0.4688	0.4150	0.3677	0.3262	0.2897	0.2575	0.2292	0.2042	0.1821	0.1625	0.1452	0.1299	0.1163	0.1042	0.0935	0.0550	0.0330
14	0.5051	0.4423	0.3878	0.3405	0.2993	0.2633	0.2320	0.2046	0.1807	0.1597	0.1413	0.1252	0.1110	0.0986	0.0876	0.0779	0.0440	0.0254
15	0.4810	0.4173	0.3625	0.3152	0.2745	0.2394	0.2090	0.1827	0.1599	0.1401	0.1229	0.1079	0.0949	0.0835	0.0736	0.0649	0.0352	0.0195
16	0.4581	0.3937	0.3387	0.2919	0.2519	0.2176	0.1883	0.1631	0.1415	0.1229	0.1069	0.0930	0.0811	0.0708	0.0618	0.0541	0.0281	0.0150
17	0.4363	0.3714	0.3166	0.2703	0.2311	0.1978	0.1696	0.1456	0.1252	0.1078	0.0929	0.0802	0.0693	0.0600	0.0520	0.0451	0.0225	0.0116
18	0.4155	0.3503	0.2959	0.2503	0.2120	0.1799	0.1528	0.1300	0.1108	0.0946	0.0808	0.0691	0.0592	0.0508	0.0437	0.0376	0.0180	0.0089
19	0.3957	0.3305	0.2765	0.2317	0.1945	0.1635	0.1377	0.1161	0.0981	0.0829	0.0703	0.0596	0.0506	0.0431	0.0367	0.0313	0.0144	0.0068
20	0.3769	0.3118	0.2584	0.2146	0.1784	0.1486	0.1240	0.1037	0.0868	0.0728	0.0611	0.0514	0.0433	0.0365	0.0308	0.0261	0.0115	0.0053

e. NET PRESENT VALUE (NPV)

Discounted cash flow can be used with the NPV method for evaluating investment proposals. For example, Sample #14 gives five-year projections of savings and costs for a new machine for Harry's Wholesale. The machine cost $5,000.

The estimate of the future savings and expenses is the most difficult part of the exercise. Harry is forecasting for five years ahead. Obviously, the longer the period of time, the less accurate the estimates are likely to be. Note that Harry's depreciation expense is calculated as follows:

Initial cost	$5,000
Less: trade-in	(1,000)
	$4,000

Depreciation (straight line) $\frac{\$4,000}{5}$ = $800/year

Depreciation is deductible as an expense for the calculation of income tax, although it does not require an outlay of cash year by year. Therefore, in order to convert Harry's annual net saving from the investment to a cash situation, the depreciation is added back each year.

Note also that there is a negative cash flow in year 1. The trade-in value is a partial recovery of the initial investment and is therefore added as a positive cash flow at the end of year 5 in Sample #14.

The data Harry is interested in from Sample #14 are the initial investment and the annual net cash flow figures. These figures have been transferred by Harry to Sample #15 and, using the relevant 10% discount factors from Sample #13, have been converted to a net present value basis. Note how Harry handled the negative cash flow figure in year 1.

Harry saw from Sample #15 that the NPV figure is positive. It is possible for an NPV figure to be negative if the initial investment exceeds the sum of the individual years' present values. In the case of negative NPV, the

SAMPLE #14
CALCULATION OF ANNUAL NET CASH FLOWS

	Year 1	Year 2	Year 3	Year 4	Year 5
Wage saving	$4,000	$4,000	$4,000	$4,000	4,000
Expenses:					
Training cost	$3,500				
Maintenance	400	$ 400	$ 400	$ 400	$ 400
Overhaul			400		
Stationery	600	600	600	600	600
Depreciation	800	800	800	800	800
Total	$5,300	$1,800	$2,200	$1,800	$1,800
Saving less expenses	($1,300)	$2,200	$1,800	$2,200	$2,200
Income tax 50%	0	$1,100	900	1,100	1,100
Net savings	($1,300)	$1,100	$ 900	$1,100	$1,100
Add: depreciation	800	800	800	800	800
trade-in					$1,100
Net cash flow	($ 500)	$1,900	$1,700	$1,900	$2,900

SAMPLE #15
NET PRESENT VALUE

Year	Net cash flow	Discount factor	Present value
1	($ 500)	0.9091	($ 455)
2	1900	0.8264	1,570
3	1700	0.7513	1,277
4	1900	0.6830	1,298
5	2900	0.6209	1,801
		Total present value	$5,491
		Initial investment	5,000
		Net present value	$ 491

investment should not be undertaken since, assuming the accuracy of the figures, the investment will not produce the rate of return desired.

Finally, the discount rate actually used should be realistic. It is frequently the rate that the owners' expect the business to earn, after taxes, on their equity investment.

f. INTERNAL RATE OF RETURN (IRR)

As we have seen, the NPV method uses a specific discount rate to determine if proposals result in a net present value greater than zero. Those that do not are rejected.

The IRR method also uses the discounted cash flow concept. However, this method's approach determines the interest (discount) rate that will make the total discounted cash inflows equal the initial investment.

For example, suppose Beth's Boutique decided to investigate renting a building adjacent to the present business in order to increase sales. Beth's investigation showed that it would cost $200,000 to renovate and equip the building with a guaranteed five-year lease. Beth's projected cash flow (net profit after tax, with depreciation added back) for each of the five years is:

Year	Cash flow
1	$ 36,000
2	40,000
3	44,000
4	50,000
5	60,000
	$230,000

In addition to the total of $230,000 cash recovery over the five years, Beth estimated the equipment could be sold for $20,000 at the end of the lease period. The total cash recovery is therefore $230,000 + $20,000 = $250,000, which is $50,000 more than the initial investment required of $200,000.

On the face of it, Beth would seem to be ahead of the game. However, if the annual flows are discounted back to their NPV, a different picture emerges, as Beth has calculated in Sample #16 which shows that the future flows of cash discounted back to today's values using a 12% rate are less than the initial investment by over $27,000. Thus, Beth knows that, if the projections about the venture are correct, there will not be a 12% cash return on the investment.

However, Beth can use the IRR method to determine the return that will be earned if the investment is made. From Sample #16 she knows that 12% is too high. By moving to a lower rate of interest, she will eventually, by trial and error, arrive at one where the NPV (the difference between total present value and initial investment) is virtually zero. Beth has calculated in Sample #17 that this is arrived at with a 7% interest (discount) rate.

Sample #17 tells Beth that the initial $200,000 investment will return the initial cash outlay except for about $300 and earn 7% on the investment. Or, stated slightly differently, Beth would recover the full $200,000 but earn slightly less than 7% interest. If she is satisfied with a 7% cash return on the investment (note this is 7% after income tax), then she would go ahead with the project.

g. NONQUANTIFIABLE BENEFITS

In this chapter we have looked at various methods of making investment decisions. We have ignored information that is not easily quantifiable but that might still be relevant to decision-making. In practice you should not ignore such factors as prestige, goodwill, reputation, employee and customer acceptance, and the social or environmental implications of investment decisions.

For example, if a business redecorates its reception area, what are the cash benefits? They may be difficult to quantify, but to retain customer goodwill the reception area may have to be decorated. Similarly, how are the relative benefits to be assessed in spending $5,000 on reception employees? Personal judgment must come into play in such decisions.

SAMPLE #16
NET PRESENT VALUE

Year	Annual cash flow	Discount factor 12%	Present value
1	$36 000	0.8929	$ 32,144
2	40 000	0.7972	31,888
3	44 000	0.7118	31,319
4	50 000	0.6355	31,775
5	60 000	0.5674	34,044
5	20 000 (trade-in)	0.5674	11,348
	Total present value		$ 172,518
	Initial investment		200,000
	Net present value		$ (27,482)

SAMPLE #17
INTERNAL RATE OF RETURN

Year	Annual cash flow	Discount factor 7%	Present value
1	$36,000	0.9346	$ 33,646
2	40,000	0.8734	34,936
3	44,000	0.8163	35,917
4	50,000	0.7629	38,145
5	60,000	0.7130	42,780
5	20,000 (trade-in)	0.7130	14,260
	Total present value		$199,684
	Initial investment		200,000
	Net present value		($ 316)

12

LEASING

One thing you must consider when starting a new business or expanding a successful existing one (unless you have a lot of money to invest) is whether or not to buy land and construct a building or buy land and/or an existing building.

Generally, most first time business owners invest far too much money in bricks and mortar (the building) when they should be leasing that asset, particularly in the early years. To a lesser degree the same is true of equipment and fixtures.

It is in the early years that the risk is often the greatest, and you may not be able to afford the heavy mortgage debt load that owning land and/or a building and expensive equipment obliges. In fact, many leases can be arranged that allow a later purchase option.

However, there may be exceptions. For example, to establish a franchised business the franchisor may insist that you own a freestanding building. In such situations the franchisor ought to be able to provide the financing, or help in finding financing.

a. LAND AND BUILDING LEASE

A lease is basically a partnership agreement between the landlord (the owner of the land and/or building) and the tenant.

There is invariably a very direct relationship between the amount of rent charged for business premises and the pedestrian or traffic count — the higher the count the higher the rent.

However, a low rent location can sometimes be overcome by spending more on advertising. But if the amount spent on advertising is greater than the rent saving there is obviously no net benefit in choosing that location.

If your business is such that the customer must find you, you should rent premises that are easy to find and easy to reach.

1. Bare leases

When checking out rentable premises, do more than look at the space and determine how large the square foot area is. See if the walls, floor, and ceiling are finished. If not, find out who pays to put the premises in rentable condition.

Some premises, even in shopping centers, are rented as bare leases. Premises rented this way are referred to as a "shell." Generally the utilities are brought only to the walls (stubbed in).

You pay for all inside finishing including lighting, plumbing, window coverings, and heating and air conditioning equipment. Determine in advance how much this is going to cost so that there are no unhappy surprises.

It is normal that any special inside finishing is your responsibility. However, if you are going to do any extensive internal remodelling that would subsequently benefit the landlord when your lease expires, see if you can negotiate a reduced rent.

2. Lease agreements

There is no standard form of lease agreement. Each lease agreement must be prepared by the lawyers of the two parties involved depending on the particular circumstances of the situation.

The agreement should cover such matters as the length of the contract (for example, 5, 10, or even 20 or more years), the amount of rent and frequency of payment, the responsibility of the two parties for the maintenance of the property, and who pays which costs for major items, such as plumbing, electrical, air conditioning, or minor items, such as cleaning and cleaning supplies. Other items of cost such as building alterations, property taxes, and insurance should also be in the agreement.

3. Expense pass-throughs

Some lease contracts contain expense pass-throughs. In other words some of the landlord's "normal" expenses become the responsibility of the tenant.

The most common pass-through is known as a triple net lease in which the tenant pays for all maintenance, property taxes, and building insurance. This can have a double effect. Any remodelling you do (such as building improvements) increases the value of the building and will thus increase your property taxes, even though you don't own the building.

Similarly, businesses in the area may be assessed a special property tax for improved community lighting, sewers, or other works. As a tenant under triple net you will pay that added burden.

Read the contract carefully, and have your lawyer go over it since some leases state that if you attach anything to the floors, walls, or ceilings it becomes the property of the lessor. This means that you could invest several thousand dollars in shelving, special lighting, equipment fixed to the floor, and so on, and as soon as you install it it is no longer legally yours.

4. Restrictions

Check the contract carefully to see if there are any landlord imposed restrictions on your business operations, such as restrictions on subletting, which you may want to do if the business is not successful and your lease still has some time to run.

The landlord should not have the right to unreasonably withhold your right to sublet, assign, or mortgage your lease, or even sell it for its remaining life, including options (see next page) to someone else. If your business is successful, the right to sell its goodwill for a profit can be quite valuable to you.

Measure your floor space so that, if rent is based on square foot area, you will not be charged for more space than you have. However, note that in some shopping malls "your" space includes a share of common areas such as halls, storage areas, elevators, and similar areas. Find out in advance what your share of this common space is.

5. Renewal option

An initial relatively short contract with one or more renewal options is often preferable to a long-term lease contract. Renewal options prevent you from being locked in if the business is not successful, but allow you to continue if it is a profitable enterprise. Any renewal options and their terms should be written into the initial contract.

In some older buildings in a city core landlords may be very reluctant to include options since they never know when an offer may come along from an investor wishing to tear down the building and construct a new one. Your successful business with two or three renewals could be in the way of the landlord.

6. Fixtures and equipment

The typical lease is generally only for the land and building, with the lessee (operator) purchasing and owning the fixtures and equipment.

If the equipment and similar items are owned by the lessor (in which case the lease payments will generally be higher), the lease agreement should specify how frequently these items are to be replaced and at whose cost.

If you own the equipment and similar items, the lease contract should provide for the disposition of them at the end of the lease period.

The two most common arrangements are that you are responsible for complete removal of such items at your cost, or that the lessor has the right to buy them at some stipulated value.

7. Contingencies

Make sure any necessary contingencies are in the contract. Contingencies might be that the contract is dependent on your obtaining necessary financing for equipment purchases or that all necessary government licenses, permits, and variances are approved. Finally, a contingency that you may inspect the site to see that it conforms to the lease description should be included.

b. RENTAL ARRANGEMENTS

With any form of lease operation, it is normal for you to bear the burden of any operating losses, although, depending on the lease arrangement, some of the net profit may have to be shared with the lessor under certain circumstances.

There are a variety of rental arrangement possibilities with leasing. Some of these are:

1. Fixed rental

A fixed rental arrangement calls for straight payments during the term of the lease. The payment might be a stepped one that increases, for example, year by year during the term of the lease. However, the payments are not variable with, and do not depend on, your sales or profits.

The lease agreement will probably allow renegotiation of the fixed amount of rent during the life of the agreement, particularly if the life is for an extended number of years.

2. Variable rental

A variable rental has a fixed portion, usually at least sufficient to give the landlord cash flow to amortize loan obligations, cover expenses, and provide a return on investment.

In addition, there will be additional rent based either on your gross sales or on your net profit.

The variable rent portion gives the landlord some hedge against inflation, although there might be a ceiling rent amount stated in the contract.

3. Percentage of sales

Another possibility is for rent to be based on sales. If so, what is to be included in sales should be completely spelled out. For example, is rental income from a cigarette vending machine located in your business's reception area to be included in sales?

Most contracts allow for a declining percentage as sales increase. For example, rent may be 6% of sales up to a certain level, then decline to 5% for any sales above that level.

Some contracts call for an increasing percentage of sales as sales increase — an escalation clause. This can be risky for you since the accelerating percentage can seriously erode normal net profit margins as sales continue to climb.

4. Percentage of profit

When rent is partly based on percentage of sales, the landlord is in a type of partnership arrangement with you. With the variable portion of rent based on profit, this partnership becomes even more firm. The profit must be carefully defined in the lease contract as either profit before income tax, profit before interest and tax, or profit before depreciation, interest, and tax.

In some lease contracts, to protect the landlord, the amount of certain types of expenses may be limited. For example, if your salary is not limited, you could pay yourself such an inflated amount that there would be no profit to be shared with the landlord by way of rent.

In other cases the contract may specify a minimum expense amount that you must spend each year, for example, for advertising so that sufficient sales and profit are generated or for maintenance so that the building is kept in good condition.

c. SALE-LEASEBACK

One other type of lease arrangement is the sale-leaseback. This occurs when a building owner sells the land to a land investor and agrees to lease it back for a number of years.

Alternatively, the owner may sell both land and the building to a property investor and contract to lease both of them back in order to be able to continue to operate the business.

If you are starting a new business or wish to expand an existing one in ideal premises that you are unable to obtain a lease on (since the owner wishes to sell the building or the building and land), it may be advisable to seek a sale-leaseback arrangement. You might be able to arrange in advance with a third party that, at the time of the purchase, these assets will be immediately sold to that third party under a leaseback arrangement to you.

Under some sale-leaseback arrangements you may also be able to structure the contract so that, at the end of the lease period, you regain ownership of the building and/or land.

d. ADVANTAGES OF LEASING

Some advantages of leasing are:

(a) Under a lease arrangement you have the obvious advantage of not having to provide capital to buy the property. Any capital you might have is then available for investment elsewhere.

(b) Your borrowing power is freed up to raise money, if required, for more critical areas of the business.

(c) Lease payments on a building are generally fully tax deductible.

(d) Owned land is not depreciable for tax purposes, but the cost of leasing land is tax deductible.

(e) Any leasehold improvements that you make to the building are generally amortized over the life of the lease rather than over the life of the building. The lease period is normally less than the building life therefore providing a tax saving.

(f) You may have a purchase option at the end of the lease period when it may be desirable to buy the land and/or building and cash is available to do this.

(g) If and when the time comes to sell the business, it may be easier to do if there is no real estate involved.

(h) Although you would not normally have this in mind when entering a lease transaction, in case of unexpected bankruptcy, you would probably only be liable for one year's rent rather than long-term mortgage payments on a property you purchased.

(i) Finally, it may be possible to arrange a lease with rental payments adjusted to the business's seasonal cash flows, even though total annual rent would be the same amount.

e. DISADVANTAGES OF LEASING

Some disadvantages of leasing are:

(a) Any capital gain in the assets accrues to the landlord and not to you. In a similar way, at the expiry of the lease, the value of the future profit of the business that you have worked hard to build up does not benefit you unless the lease is renewed.

(b) The cost of a lease may be higher than some other form of financing.

(c) It may also be more difficult for you to borrow money with leased premises if there are no assets (other than a lease agreement) to pledge as collateral.

(d) Finally, the total cash outflow in rental payments may be greater in the long run than for purchasing the property.

f. RENTAL AGENTS

If you are negotiating a lease through a rental agent, remember that the agent has only one mandate: to rent empty space for the landlord as quickly as possible to earn a commission.

You should know more about what you want for your particular business than the agent. In other words, be prepared by arming yourself in advance with as many facts as possible about the type and particularly the size of premises you need.

Also, be alert to agents whose main motivation is to rent you less than adequate premises, particularly in a poor location for your type of business.

g. EQUIPMENT LEASE

Consider also the possibility of leasing any needed fixtures and equipment in order to lower your start-up costs.

Some sites, since they were previously occupied by a business similar to yours, may come already equipped with usable equipment and furnishings.

In other cases, since the premises are a shell, you will have to find your own equipment and furnishings. Some suppliers of equipment will lease directly. In other cases you will lease from a company that specializes in leasing and has bought the equipment from the supplier. The supplier may act as an intermediary in such cases.

Most equipment leases cannot be cancelled and require you to make a series of payments whose total sum will exceed the cost of assets if purchased outright, since the lessor has to make a profit on his or her investment.

Depreciation of the assets is the lessor's prerogative as owner of the assets. Maintenance is usually, but not invariably, a cost of the lessor.

Generally, the lessor owns any residual value in the assets, although contracts sometimes give you the right to purchase the assets at your option, at a specified price, at the end of the lease period. In such cases the lease purchase is actually a type of conditional sale and you have any tax advantages that claiming expenses such as depreciation may offer.

In some cases you will also have the option to renew the lease for a specified further period.

1. Advantages of equipment leasing

There are some advantages to leasing equipment. Flexibility is considered to be an advantage because you avoid the risk of obsolescence you might otherwise have if the assets are purchased outright. However, the lessor probably considers the cost of obsolescence when the lease rates are determined.

You also avoid the problems of maintenance and its cost. However, the lessor will normally build the cost of maintenance into the lease payments.

If no down payment is required, 100% financing of leased assets may be possible. For relatively short-lived assets like equipment and fixtures this is an advantage even if you have the cash to pay for them outright. This cash is then free for investment in longer-lived assets, such as land or building, that frequently appreciate in value as time goes by. Equipment depreciates very rapidly and usually has little or no residual value.

Finally, income tax is an important consideration. Since lease payments are generally fully tax deductible, there can be an advantage in leasing. On the other hand, if you are an owner you can deduct for income tax purposes both depreciation and the interest expense on any debt financing of the purchase. However, what might be an advantage with one lease arrangement may be a disadvantage with another. Each situation must be considered on its own merits as far as tax implications are concerned.

A sale-leaseback of equipment is also not uncommon. You simply sell your equipment to a bank, finance company, or even a leasing firm at a price close to its current market value and then lease it back for its remaining usable life. However, the lease costs may be comparatively high since the lessor receives little or no tax benefit (for example, through depreciation) for owning used equipment. In addition there may be sales or use taxes on the transaction.

2. Disadvantages of equipment leasing

A disadvantage of leasing equipment is that any money borrowed to make the lease payments can be more expensive by an interest point or more than money borrowed to purchase the equipment outright.

Also, the lessor is the owner of the equipment and has the right to repossess it if you do not meet the payments. If you owned the equipment, you would not lose any residual value remaining in the equipment.

h. EFFECT ON FINANCIAL RATIOS

In chapter 2 financial ratios were discussed. In that chapter it was assumed that all assets were owned. If any are leased, particularly major ones like land, building, and equipment, there can be a considerable effect on certain key financial ratios.

With a lease arrangement, the net fixed assets, the long-term debt, and the owner's equity on the balance sheet will all be reduced. On the income statement, even though total sales do not change, certain expenses such as depreciation, interest, property taxes, and maintenance will be much less while there will be an additional expense for leasing.

Consider the following two alternative situations, one where land and building are owned, and the other where they are leased:

BALANCE SHEETS

	Own	Lease
Current assets	$ 50,000	$ 50,000
Fixed assets	500,000	100,000
Total assets	$550,000	$150,000
Current liabilities	$ 30,000	$ 30,000
Long-term debt	360,000	60,000
Total liabilities	$390,000	$ 90,000
Owner's equity	160,000	60,000
Total liabilities and equity	$550,000	$150,000

INCOME STATEMENTS

	Own	Lease
Sales	$500,000	$500,000
Profit before lease expense	$ 12,000	$ 49,000
Lease expense	0	33,000
Profit before tax	$ 12,000	$ 16,000
Income tax 50%	6,000	8,000
Net profit	$ 6,000	$ 8,000

From these financial statements certain ratios can be calculated:

	Own	Lease
Net profit to sales	1.2%	1.6%
Net profit to assets	1.1%	5.3%
Debt to equity ratio	2.44:1	1.5:1
Return on equity	3.75%	13.33%

The net profit to sales has increased as has the net profit to assets, while the debt to equity ratio has declined implying that this is a better credit risk situation that would make it easier to borrow additional funds.

However, these "improved" ratios may be misleading since any long-term lease payments contracted for should be considered just as much a long-term obligation to the business as mortgage payments are in an ownership of those assets.

Note that, in this illustration, the return on equity has been considerably improved. If this were an actual situation that alone might be sufficient justification to lease, rather than own, those assets.

However, in an actual situation it might be a good idea to use an investment analysis method, such as NPV discussed in chapter 11, to better evaluate your final decision.

i. A CASE SITUATION

To illustrate how to make a purchase versus lease comparison using NPV, consider the following facts.

Dizzy's Distribution company is considering the purchase for $250,000 of the vehicles it needs. Since Dizzy has a well established record with his bank he can borrow the entire $250,000 required. The loan will be repayable in four equal annual installments of principal ($62,500 a year) plus interest at 8%. The vehicles will be depreciated over five years at $50,000 a year. They are assumed to have no trade-in value at the end of that period. Dizzy's company is in a 50% tax bracket.

As an alternative to purchasing, Dizzy can lease the delivery vehicles at a rental cost of $60,000 a year.

Dizzy's first step, with the purchase proposal, is to prepare a bank loan repayment schedule showing principal and interest payments for each of the four years of the loan. This is illustrated in Sample #18.

Dizzy next calculates the net cash outflow for each of the five years as in Sample #19. In this sample note that, since depreciation and the bank loan interest expense are tax deductible, and since Dizzy's company is in a 50% tax bracket, there is an annual income tax saving equal to 50% of the total of those two expenses.

Thus, in year 1, the expenses of $70,000 are offset by the $35,000 tax saving. The net cost, after tax, is therefore only $35,000. This $35,000 cost has to be increased by the principal repayment on the loan of $62,500, and reduced by the depreciation expense of $50,000 (since depreciation does not require an outlay of cash). The result for Dizzy is that, in year 1, the net cash outflow is $47,500.

Dizzy calculated net cash outflow figures in a similar way for the other four years and noted that in year 5, since the bank loan has been paid off, there is no interest and bank loan payment to be adjusted for. For this reason the net cash flow is positive (because $25,000 less is paid in income tax than would otherwise be the case) rather than negative.

Sample #20 shows Dizzy's calculation of the annual net cash outflows under the rental option. Note that, with this option, there is no depreciation expense since the company does not own the vehicles and no interest or principal payments since no money is to be borrowed.

Finally, Dizzy transferred the net cash flow figures from Samples #19 and #20 to Sample #21 and discounted them back using an appropriate discount factor (in Dizzy's case 8%, since that was the interest rate to be paid on borrowed money) using the discount factors from Sample #14. Sample #21 shows Dizzy that, from a present value point of view it would be better to rent in this particular case, since total present value of the cash outflows is lower by $8,903 ($128,681 - $119,778).

SAMPLE #18
BANK LOAN REPAYMENT SCHEDULE

Year	Interest at 8%	Principal amount	Balance
0			$250,000
1	$20,000	$62,500	187,500
2	15,000	62,500	125,000
3	10,000	62,500	62,500
4	5,000	62,500	0

The decision in Dizzy's case to lease does not mean that the decision will always be to lease. The many variables involved can change from situation to situation. For this reason each case must be judged on its own merits.

For example, in a purchase plan, a company might use some of its own cash as a down payment and thus borrow less from the bank. Also, under a purchase plan, there might be a trade-in value of the equipment at the end of its useful life.

Further, with a lease, there might be a purchase option to the lessee at the end of the period and, if the purchase option is to be exercised, this additional cash outflow at that time must be considered.

Finally, the terms on borrowed money can change from time to time, and different methods of depreciation can be used. For example, the use of an accelerated depreciation method will give higher depreciation expense in the earlier years, thus reducing income tax and increasing the cash flow in those years.

Because of all these and even other possibilities, each purchase versus lease situation must be investigated on its own merits, using all the known variables in the calculations before you make your final decision.

SAMPLE #19
ANNUAL NET CASH OUTFLOW WITH PURCHASE

	Year 1	Year 2	Year 3	Year 4	Year 5
Interest expense (from Sample #18)	$20,000	$15,500	$10,000	$ 5,000	0
Depreciation expense	50,000	50,000	50,000	50,000	$ 50,000
Total tax deductible expense	$70,000	$65,000	$60,000	$55,000	$50,000
Income tax saving 50%	(35,000)	(32,500)	(30,000)	(27,500)	(25,000)
After tax cost	$35,000	$32,500	$30,000	$27,500	$25,000
Add: principal payments	62,500	62,500	62,500	62,500	0
Deduct: depreciation	(50,000)	(50,000)	(50,000)	(50,000)	(50,000)
Net cash outflow (inflow)	$47,500	$45,000	$42,500	$40,000	($25,000)

SAMPLE #20
ANNUAL NET CASH OUTFLOW WITH RENTAL

	Year 1	Year 2	Year 3	Year 4	Year 5
Rent expense	$60,000	$60,000	$60,000	$60,000	$60,000
Income tax saving 50%	(30,000)	(30,000)	(30,000)	(30,000)	(30,000)
Net cash outflow	$30,000	$30,000	$30,000	$30,000	$30,000

SAMPLE #21
TOTAL PRESENT VALUE OF PURCHASE VERSUS RENT

	PURCHASE			RENT		
Year	Annual cash outflow (inflow)	Discount factor 8%	Present value	Annual cash outflow	Discount factor 8%	Present value
1	$47,500	0.9259	$43,980	$30,000	0.9259	$27,777
2	45,000	0.8573	38,579	30,000	0.8573	25,719
3	42,500	0.7938	33,737	30,000	0.7938	23,814
4	40,000	0.7350	29,400	30,000	0.7350	22,050
5	(25,000)	0.6806	(17,015)	30,000	0.6806	20,418
	Total present value		$128,681	Total present value		$119,778

CANADIAN

ORDER FORM

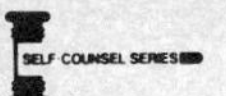

SELF-COUNSEL SERIES

8/84

NATIONAL TITLES:

	Title	Price
_____	Adopted?	3.95
_____	Advertising for Small Business	4.95
_____	Assertiveness for Managers	8.95
_____	Basic Accounting	5.95
_____	Becoming a Canadian	3.50
_____	Better Book for Getting Hired	9.95
_____	Business Guide to Telephone Systems	7.95
_____	Buying (and Selling) a Small Business	6.95
_____	Changing Your Name in Canada	3.50
_____	Civil Rights	8.95
_____	Collection Techniques for the Small Business	4.95
_____	Complete Guide to Being Your Own Home Contractor	19.95
_____	Credit, Debt, and Bankruptcy	5.95
_____	Criminal Procedure in Canada	12.95
_____	Drinking and Driving	4.50
_____	Editing Your Newsletter	14.95
_____	Exporting	12.50
_____	Federal Incorporation and Business Guide	12.95
_____	Financial Control for the Small Business	5.95
_____	Financial Freedom on $5 A Day	6.95
_____	For Sale By Owner	4.95
_____	Franchising in Canada	5.95
_____	Fundraising	5.50
_____	Getting Money	14.95
_____	Getting Sales	14.95
_____	Getting Started	11.95
_____	How You Too Can Make a Million . . . In the Mail Order Business	8.95
_____	Immigrating to Canada	12.95
_____	Immigrating to the U.S.A.	12.95
_____	Importing	21.95
_____	Insuring Business Risks	3.50
_____	Learn to Type Fast	6.50
_____	Life Insurance for Canadians	3.50
_____	Managing Your Office Records and Files	14.95
_____	Media Law Handbook	6.50
_____	Mike Grenby's Tax Tips	5.95
_____	Mike Grenby's Money Book	5.50
_____	Money Spinner	14.95
_____	Mortgage and Foreclosure Handbook	5.95
_____	Parents' Guide to Day Care	5.95
_____	Public Speaking	4.95
_____	Resort Condos	4.50
_____	Runaway Inflation	2.95
_____	Retirement Guide for Canadians	8.95
_____	Start and Run a Profitable Beauty Salon	14.95
_____	Start and Run a Profitable Craft Business	10.95
_____	Start and Run a Profitable Home Typing Business	9.95
_____	Start and Run a Profitable Restaurant	10.95
_____	Start and Run a Profitable Retail Business	11.95
_____	Start and Run a Profitable Video Store	10.95
_____	Starting a Successful Business in Canada	12.95
_____	Tax Law Handbook	11.95
_____	Taxpayer Alert!	4.95
_____	Tax Shelters in Canada	6.95
_____	Trusts and Trust Companies	3.95
_____	Using the Access to Information Act	5.95
_____	Word Processing	8.95
_____	Working Couples	5.50
_____	Write Right!	(Cloth) 5.95 / (Paper) 4.95

PROVINCIAL TITLES:
Please indicate which provincial edition is required.

Consumer Book
☐B.C. 7.95 ☐Ontario 6.95

SELF COUNSEL SERIES

8/84

AMERICAN ORDER FORM SELF-COUNSEL SERIES

NATIONAL TITLES

	Title	Price
______	Assertiveness for Managers	8.95
______	Basic Accounting for the Small Business	4.50
______	Business Guide to Telephone Systems	7.95
______	Buying (and Selling) a Small Business	6.95
______	Collection Techniques for the Small Business	4.95
______	Exporting from the U.S.A.	12.95
______	Financial Control for the Small Business	5.50
______	Financial Freedom on $5 a Day	5.95
______	Fundraising for Non-Profit Groups	5.50
______	Franchising in the U.S.	5.95
______	Getting Sales	14.95
______	Immigrating to Canada	12.95
______	Immigrating to the U.S.A.	12.95
______	Learn to Type Fast	6.50
______	The Money Spinner	14.95
______	Parents' Guide to Day Care	5.95
______	Resort Condos & Time Sharing	4.50
______	Retirement in the Pacific Northwest	4.95
______	Start and Run a Profitable Beauty Salon	14.95
______	Start and Run a Profitable Craft Business	10.95
______	Start and Run a Profitable Home Typing Business	9.95
______	Start and Run a Profitable Home Typing Business	9.95
______	Start and Run a Profitable Restaurant	10.95
______	Start and Run a Profitable Retail Store	11.95
______	Start and Run a Profitable Video Store	10.95
______	Starting a Successful Business on West Coast	12.95
______	You and the Police	3.50
______	Word Processing	8.95
______	Working Couples	4.50

STATE TITLES

Please indicate which state edition is required.

______ Divorce Guide
☐ Washington (with forms) 12.95 ☐ Oregon

______ Employee/Employer Rights
☐ Washington 5.50

______ Incorporation and Business Guide
☐ Washington ☐ Oregon 11.95

BUSINESS TITLES

ASSERTIVENESS FOR MANAGERS
Valuable advice for anyone in a supervisory position is given on effective skills for managing people. Exercises are included.

ADVERTISING FOR THE SMALL BUSINESS
Tells you from start to finish how to advertise effectively even if you have never done it before. It explains the jargon and illustrates the basic principles of every medium of advertising.

BASIC ACCOUNTING FOR THE SMALL BUSINESS
Discusses day-to-day accounting problems encountered in running a small business. Instructions for preliminary bookkeeping and organizing financial matters are given.

BUSINESS GUIDE TO TELEPHONE SYSTEMS
Difficult choices are made easy in this readable guide to the communications technology. This book guides the business person through the maze of regulations, basic systems, systems management, and needs assessment.

BUYING (AND SELLING) A SMALL BUSINESS
Buying a business is often the easiest way to become an entrepreneur. This book shows how to carefully investigate the potential profitability of a business, how to assess the asking price, and how to be sure you get what you paid for.

COLLECTION TECHNIQUES FOR THE SMALL BUSINESS
When polite reminders about overdue accounts don't bring anything but polite excuses, you don't have to give up. You can use the same successful techniques that the professionals use to collect money.

FUNDRAISING FOR NON-PROFIT GROUPS

Raising money is the most essential and also the most difficult task for any organization. This book explains how to do it, from making up the budget to approaching corporation presidents and other possible funders.

GETTING SALES

Designed to serve sales people, independent retailers, small and large manufacturers, service businesses and consultants, this book provides step-by-step instructions for finding more customers and increasing sales.

GETTING STARTED

If you want to go into business for yourself, either part-time or full-time, you will need to know every sales and marketing tip there is. *Getting Started* offers tips to fight inflation, increase sales, use effective advertising, and increase the success of your business.
Available in Canada only.

LEARN TO TYPE FAST

This book provides a unique method of learning how to type. This new system, which you can learn in five hours, teaches you the keys in relation to your fingers, rather than the keyboard.

STARTING A SUCCESSFUL BUSINESS

Information regarding tax laws, purchasing an existing business, and the entire field of successful business operation is authoritatively discussed and well-explained.
Editions available for Canada and U.S. West Coast only. See order form.

WORD PROCESSING HANDBOOK

This book describes the kinds of machines available and evaluates them in terms of individual businesses and their needs. It shows how to shop for the word processor you need.

WRITE RIGHT!

The author, a professional writer and editor, shows how to write effectively with little effort. She explains when to use certain words and phrases, where the commas go, and how to say what you really mean.
Available in Canada only.

EDITING YOUR NEWSLETTER

This book is for anyone who edits a regular newsletter. It discusses how to establish the goals of your newsletter, how to distribute it, how to produce a quality item with a limited budget, and how to gather news regularly.
Available in Canada only.

EMPLOYEE/EMPLOYER GUIDE

Offers a clear explanation of labor law, including labor standards regarding age of employment, wages, hours of work, rest periods, maternity leave, and much more.
Not available for all provinces and states. See order form.

EXPORTING

Details are given about what to look for in developing export markets, what pitfalls to beware of, how to deal with foreign businesses, and how to do the tons of necessary paperwork in order to export.

IMPORTING

There are thousands of regulations and dozens of forms involved in importing, and this comprehensive guide explains what they're all about.
Available in Canada only.

INCORPORATION GUIDE

The practice and theory of establishing a private limited company, along with the principles of limited liability are outlined and clarified. Step-by-step instructions for incorporating your company are included.
Not available for all provinces and states. See order form.

FINANCIAL CONTROL FOR THE SMALL BUSINESS

In easy-to-understand language, this book takes you through the "after the basics" accounting procedure for the small business, and shows how your accounts affect your business, and how you can increase sales and success by gaining control of your books.

FRANCHISING

Buying a franchise can be a good, lower-risk way to go into business for yourself, but it is not an instant road to success. Here is an explanation of royalty terms, franchise sites, and unethical pyramid schemes. Included is a questionnaire to help the buyer identify suitable franchises and practical advice for finding a good investment.

START AND RUN SERIES

START AND RUN A PROFITABLE BEAUTY SALON

This is a comprehensive book on every aspect of operating a beauty salon. It covers everything from choosing the decor to hiring and firing staff and selling beauty products.

START AND RUN A PROFITABLE CRAFT BUSINESS

This exceptional book is for anyone who has ever considered taking up crafts, or who is already involved in crafts as a hobby, and wants to turn the hobby into a money making project.

START AND RUN A PROFITABLE HOME TYPING BUSINESS

A home typing business is an easy, covenient way to earn good money and work when you want, where you want. This helpful guide provides all the information you need to get started and to keep your business running smoothly.

START AND RUN A PROFITABLE RETAIL BUSINESS

Opening a retail store is a very different venture than opening a factory or a service business. This book explains what steps the small retailer should take and specifically deals with the unique problems and opportunities of retail stores.

START AND RUN A PROFITABLE RESTAURANT

Eight out of every ten restaurants fail or change hands in the first year of operation This book is intended to prevent that. Everything from site selection to theme and menu planning is included.

START AND RUN A PROFITABLE VIDEO STORE

The video business is booming and opening a video store is the latest way to make a fast dollar. This book guides the novice business person through the first uncertain years of running a new business in a new field.

MONEY TITLES

FINANCIAL FREEDOM ON $5 A DAY

This book guides you through a newly developed method for investors who have little capital and who want a minimum risk investment plan. A comprehensive Resource Directory of investment sources is included.

HOW YOU TOO CAN MAKE AT LEAST $1 MILLION IN THE MAIL-ORDER BUSINESS

A landmark book, it shows you how to build a mail-order business from a standing start into a property that you should be able to sell, in about five years, to a large listed corporation for at least one million dollars.

MIKE GRENBY'S MONEY BOOK

Written in a lighthearted manner, this handbook for saving money includes topics like arranging a wedding, renting versus buying accommodation, fitting out a new home and buying a car, to shopping for baby.
Available in Canada only.

MIKE GRENBY'S TAX TIPS

In this quick reference book, updated yearly, Mike Grenby tells you how to reduce your tax burden by following the simple steps he outlines.
Available in Canada only.

THE MONEY SPINNER

This book explains a low-risk, high-profit investment system. It will show, step-by-step, how you can multiply your investment several times over in the next few years.

TAX LAW HANDBOOK

This book explains how the tax law in Canada works and how you can make it work to your advantage. It is especially useful for students, accountants, lawyers, and business people who have complicated tax matters to deal with.
Available in Canada only.

TAX SHELTERS

Tax Shelters not only explains the financial workings behind RRSPs, RHOSPs, DPSPs, and MURBs, but also exposes the often-hidden hazards and pitfalls of savings plans.
Available in Canada only.

TAXPAYER ALERT!

Here is a guide to how the tax department works. It spells out your obligations, and shows who is most likely to be audited and how the auditor works. It explains just how tax avoiders are caught while others are able to avoid taxes legally.
Available in Canada only.